D1457847

EDUCATION, EQUITY
AND ECONOMIC COMPETITIVENESS
IN THE AMERICAS:
An Inter-American Dialogue Project

Volume I: Key Issues

This publication is part of the *INTERAMER* series of the General Secretariat of the Organization of American States. The ideas, thoughts, and opinions expressed are not necessarily those of the OAS nor of its Member States. The opinions expressed are the responsibility of the authors. Correspondence should be directed to the Editorial Center, Department of Educational Affairs, 1889 "F" Street, N.W., 2nd Floor, Washington, D.C., 20006, U.S.A.

EDUCATION, EQUITY AND ECONOMIC COMPETITIVENESS IN THE AMERICAS:
An Inter-American Dialogue Project

Volume I: Key Issues

JEFFREY M. PURYEAR
JOSÉ JOAQUÍN BRUNNER
Editors

INTERAMER 37
EDUCATIONAL SERIES

The editorial revision of this monograph was done by Antonio Octávio Cintra, Regional Coordinator for the Multinational Project on Secondary and Higher Education (PROMESUP) of the General Secretariat of the OAS.

Colección INTERAMER/*INTERAMER Collection*

Director/*Director, a.c.*
   Jorge D. García

Editor/*Editor*
   Carlos E. Paldao

Editor Asistente/*Assistant Editor*
   Yadira Soto

Editor de Producción/*Production Editor*
   Alison August

Composición Electrónica/*Desktop Publishing*
   Juan Carlos Gómez y Lourdes Vales

Fotografía de la Cubierta/*Cover Photograph*
   Pablo Rodríguez

Primera edición abril 1994/*First edition April 1994*
Primera reimpresión febrero 1995/*First reprint February 1995*

INTERAMER No. 37 - Serie Educativa/*Educational Series*

Library of Congress Cataloging-in-Publications Data

Education, equity and economic competitiveness in the Americas /
   Jeffrey M. Puryear and José Joaquín Brunner, editors.
            p.   cm. — (colección INTERAMER, ISSN 1021-4666 ;
      no. 37-. Serie educativa = INTERAMER collection; no. 37-.
      Educational series)
      Includes bibliographical references.
      Contents: v. 1. Key issues
   ISBN 0-8270-3314-1 (v. 1)
      1. Education—Latin America—Aims and objectives.
      2. Education—Economic aspects—Latin America. 3. Educational
      change—Latin America. 4. Economic development—Effect of
      education on. 5. Educational equalization—Latin America.
I. Puryear, Jeffrey.   II. Brunner, José Joaquín.   III. Series:
Colección INTERAMER ; no. 37- IV. Series: Colección INTERAMER.
Serie educativa.
      LA541.E2755   1994
      370'.98—dc20   94-877
                                                                CIP

This publication was produced within the framework
of the activities which are executed by the
Member States of the OAS
with the support of the
Regional Program for Educational Development
(PREDE/OAS)

The papers contained in this volume
were commissioned for the first phase
of the Task Force on Education, Equity
and Economic Competitiveness in the Americas,
a project of the Inter-American Dialogue.

TABLE OF CONTENTS

PRESENTATION

There is a tide in the affairs of men
which, taken at the flood, leads on to fortune;
omitted, all the voyage of their life
is bound in shallows and in miseries.
— William Shakespeare, *Julius Caesar*

The publication of this book coincides with a period of intense political, economic, scientific and technological change. It also happens at a time of discontent and rejection of the *status quo*, with growing demands for popular participation in decisions that until recently were made in closed circles of power. Current discourse centers on such themes as individual rights, decentralization, delegation of authority, and respect for local values and regional preferences.

The papers contained in this book discuss these and related phenomena from different perspectives. However, they are linked by their emphasis on alternative approaches to the modernization of the Hemisphere's educational systems that are increasingly associated with aspirations to equality, greater possibilities of competing in the international market and higher income.

By publishing this book, the OAS Department of Educational Affairs (DEA) contributes to the success of the projects of reform, such as the one it has been developing in conjunction with the Ministry of Education of Paraguay. The latter activity is realized within the framework of the multinational projects financed by the OAS Member States, and is characterized by a philosophy of solidary cooperation. Employees of DEA, as well as its national and international consultants, participate in the effort to better understand the operation of Paraguayan schools (and other formal or informal entities), as long as DEA collaboration is requested by that country.

It is therefore easy to understand DEA's interest in the studies and discussions on the theme of educational reform in the Americas that are promoted by the Inter-American Dialogue and by the Corporation for Research on Development (CINDE). It is also gratifying to note that some of the conclusions central to this book support the premises upon which the OAS cooperative regional programs in the areas of Education, Science and Culture are based: their complementary nature in relation to national activities; the eminently cooperative character of the projects of reform and modernization; the joint division of responsibilities in the administration of multinational projects between national and regional coordinators; the selection of the school (as well as other formal and informal mechanisms for promoting learning) as the focus of the process of change; and the attempt to disseminate the results of the projects through the *Revista Latinoamericana de Innovaciones Educativas* and *INFOCIECC* (Information System of the OAS Inter-American Council for Education, Science and Culture).

The reader who is familiar with the notion of *better* spending on education in Latin America will be surprised to learn that this is not enough. In order to modernize the learning and teaching systems of the region, it is also necessary to spend *more*, because the tax effort is relatively low in regards to educational activities. The reader may also be surprised with the assertion that technical cooperation, as practiced by some international agencies and banks, may actually aggravate the difficulties encountered by national authorities developing reform. As we strengthen our convictions about the close relationship between education, technology and development, we realize how waves of change, generated by initiatives deriving from trade and industrial policies, alter the behavior of the educational sector, sometimes in radical and unexpected ways. This book will prove that the theme of educational reform sparks the interest not only of professionals in the field, but of a much larger audience.

Getúlio P. Carvalho

EDUCATION, EQUITY AND ECONOMIC COMPETITIVENESS IN THE AMERICAS:

An Inter-American Dialogue Project

VOLUME 1: KEY ISSUES

INTRODUCTION

Few issues facing the societies of Latin America and the Caribbean are more important than educational reform. As countries shift throughout the region toward open economies, democratic governance and state decentralization, they are placing radically new demands on education systems, requiring that they train students for jobs in an internationally competitive economy, foster technological change, promote social equity and prepare people for democratic citizenship. Yet the region's traditional model of educational development—in place since the 1960s—has focused almost exclusively on expanding enrollments and has not delivered adequate levels of quality, equity and efficiency. The result has been a system that often fails to meet the demands of modern labor markets and modern citizenship, and resists change. A new approach is needed.

In an effort to address this crucial issue, the Inter-American Dialogue, in collaboration with the Corporation for Research on Development (CINDE) in Santiago, Chile, decided to establish a special Task Force on Education, Equity and Economic Competitiveness in the Americas. The Task Force is chaired by Senator José Octavio Bordón of Argentina, who earlier served as governor of the province of Mendoza, and John R. Petty, the former chairman and CEO of Marine Midland Bank and presently chairman of the Czech and Slovak American Enterprise Fund. It is composed of distinguished leaders from Latin and North America and the Caribbean, drawn from the diverse sectors—government, business, political parties, the academy, churches and professional associations—that have a stake in the region's educational systems. Its chief objective is to develop a broader and more active constituency for educational reform. Task Force activities are being codirected by Jeffrey M. Puryear and José Joaquín Brunner.

The papers presented in these two volumes were commissioned for the first phase of the Task Force program. That phase concluded on November 19, 1993 with a day-long meeting in Washington that brought together a group of prominent leaders and education specialists to shape a work plan for Task Force activities in 1994 and beyond, and to contribute to the production of a policy paper assessing the chief problems afflicting education in the region and the opportunities for constructive change. The meeting was attended by representatives of diverse sectors—government, business, political parties, education and

3

the academy—from Latin and North America and the Caribbean. Participants from the Inter-American Dialogue included Mssrs. Bordón and Petty; David Hamburg, president of the Carnegie Corporation in New York; Senator Billie Miller, opposition party leader of Barbados; and Dialogue President Peter Hakim. Others attending the meeting included Osvaldo Sunkel, director of CINDE; Juan Carlos Tedesco, director of the International Bureau of Education of the United Nations Economic Commission for Latin America and the Caribbean (UNECLAC); and representatives from the Organization of American States, the Inter-American Development Bank, the United States Agency for International Development, and the Academy of Educational Development.

The commissioned papers—four of them exploring key education policy issues and eight country-specific case studies—were intended to provide background for the discussions at the meeting. They were prepared by distinguished experts on educational reform from throughout the Americas. Among the authors of the papers were Eduardo Aldana, director of SER Research Institute in Colombia; Patricia Arregui, executive director of the Group of Analysis for Development (GRADE) in Peru; Thomas Bailey, director of the Institute on Education and the Economy at the Teachers College of Columbia University in New York; Cecilia Braslavsky, coordinator of Education and Society at the Latin American Faculty of the Social Sciences (FLASCO) in Argentina; Cristián Cox, director of the Educational Quality and Equity Improvement Program of the Chilean Ministry of Education; Joseph Farrell, professor at the Ontario Institute for Studies in Education in Canada; Carlos Filgueira, senior researcher at the Uruguayan Center for Information and Studies (CIESU) in Uruguay; Carmen García Guadilla, professor at the Center for Development Studies (CENDES) of the Central University of Venezuela; María de Ibarrola, director general of the SNTE Foundation for the Culture of the Mexican Teacher in Mexico City; and Simón Schwartzman, senior researcher at the Nucleus for Research on Higher Education (NUPES) at the University of São Paulo in Brazil.

The four papers published in volume one address themes that are currently central in the debate over educational reform: the economic and technological context of educational change; the allocation of public funds across educational levels; the requirements for developing effective schools; and the role of foreign assistance in facilitating reform of education systems. Several conclusions in these four papers merit special attention: 1) that the competitiveness of firms and nations depends increasingly on the relationships between education, business and technological development; 2) that in order to carry out comprehensive educational reform, the countries of the region need both to increase their investments in human resources and to manage those funds more efficiently; 3) that such changes will only produce the desired effects if they manage to improve the processes of teaching and learning that take place at the classroom level; and 4) that successfully promoting educational reform requires solid knowledge regarding local conditions and constant feedback among the several stages of policy development—analysis, formulation, implementation and evaluation— a process that can be strengthened through new forms of foreign assistance and cooperation.

Volume two presents eight country-specific case studies analyzing entire education systems from preschool to tertiary. Here the emphasis is on briefly describing the fundamental characteristics of the education systems in each country, identifying their principal problems in terms of equity, quality and efficiency, and documenting the efforts at change currently underway. Each paper also compares the national education agenda with the recommendations presented in the recent publication—*Education and Knowledge: Basic Pillars of Changing Production Patterns with Social Equity*—by the Economic Commission for Latin America and the Caribbean (ECLAC) and the United Nations Education, Science and Culture Organization (UNESCO).

During phase two of the project, the Task Force will develop and administer a program of activities in coordination with national teams established in approximately six Latin American and Caribbean countries. These activities will culminate in the preparation of a comprehensive, high-profile report that makes the case for education reform, lays out the principal issues, and makes policy recommendations, along with a diversified program of analysis, consultations, publications and outreach.

Funding for the papers, the conference and for other activities carried out during phase one of the Inter-American Dialogue Task Force was provided by the Canadian International Development Research Centre (IDRC), the United States Agency for International Development (USAID) and the Swedish International Development Agency (SIDA).

Jeffrey M. Puryear
José Joaquín Brunner

EFFECTIVE CLASSROOMS, EFFECTIVE SCHOOLS: A RESEARCH BASE FOR REFORM IN LATIN AMERICAN EDUCATION

Robert E. Slavin[*]

SUMMARY

This paper describes the requirements for effective reform in education. At the classroom level, successful reform depends on a focus on four factors: quality of instruction, levels of instruction appropriate to student needs, incentives for students, and adequate time for learning. Research on means of enhancing each of these factors is reviewed. Requirements for school effectiveness and school change are reviewed, and these are discussed in the Latin American context. The paper concludes that the key to school improvement in Latin America will be professional development focusing on whole-school change, including adoption of proven methods and materials on a schoolwide basis. Effective change is most likely to be comprehensive, systemic, and sustained, with school staffs taking an active role in choosing from among effective alternatives. At the system level, school-by-school change must begin small and expand rapidly with support from all levels of school administration.

---

[*]   Robert Slavin is currently Director of the Early and Elementary School Program at the Center for Research on Effective Schooling for Disadvantaged Students at Johns Hopkins University. He received his B.A. in Psychology from Reed College in 1972, and his Ph.D. in Social Relations in 1975 from Johns Hopkins University. Dr. Slavin has authored or co-authored more than 140 articles and 14 books, including *Educational Psychology: Theory into Practice* (Allyn and Bacon 1986, 1988, 1991, 1994), *School and Classroom Organization* (Erlbaum 1989), *Effective Programs for Students at Risk* (Allyn and Bacon 1989), *Cooperative Learning: Theory, Research, and Practice* (Prentice-Hall 1990), and *Preventing Early School Failure* (Allyn and Bacon, forthcoming). He received the American Educational Research Association's Raymond B. Cattell Early Career Award for Programmatic Research in 1986, and the Palmer O. Johnson award for the best article in an AERA journal in 1988.

Introduction

Education has always been a critical requirement for economic development, but as the world economy is changing, education is becoming increasingly important. Natural resources, location, and other factors are declining in importance as the ability of a nation's people to do complex work is becoming the key determinant of national wealth. Nations throughout the world have long been aware of the link between education and prosperity and are seeking to improve their educational systems. Increasing investment in education is one focus in many countries, but there is no guarantee that increasing funding will result in increased student performance. What matters is what schools and school systems do with existing or increased funds to increase the efficacy of teaching and learning.

The most important dynamic in education is the interaction between teacher and child. Every other element of the education system merely provides the context within which teacher-child interaction takes place. A discussion of school reform must begin with a discussion of the teaching behaviors and school characteristics associated with optimum student achievement, and then build up from there a system to support these behaviors and characteristics.

The purpose of this paper is to summarize research on effective teaching and effective schools, and to then relate this research to policies and practices that might be involved in the reform of schools in Latin America and elsewhere.

Effective Teaching

In the past twenty years, research on teaching has made significant strides in identifying teaching behaviors associated with high student achievement (Brophy and Good 1986; Rosenshine and Stevens 1986). However, effective instruction is not just good teaching. If it were, we could probably find the best lecturers, make video tapes of their lessons, and show them to students (see Slavin 1987a, 1994). Consider why the video teacher would be ineffective. First, the video teacher would have no idea what students already know. A particular lesson might be too advanced for a particular group of students, or it may be that some students already know the material being taught. Some students may be learning the lesson quite well, while others are missing key concepts and falling behind because they lack prerequisite skills for new learning. The video teacher would have no way to know who needed additional help, and would have no way to provide it in any case. There would be no way to question students to find out if they were getting the main points and then to reteach any concepts students were failing to grasp.

Second, the video teacher would have no way to motivate students to pay attention to the lesson or to really try to learn it. If students were failing to pay attention or were misbehaving, the video teacher would have no way of doing anything about it. Finally, the video teacher would never know at the end of the lesson whether or not students actually learned the main concepts or skills.

The case of the video teacher illustrates the point that teachers must be concerned with many elements of instruction in addition to the lesson itself. Teachers must attend to ways of adapting instruction to students' levels of knowledge, motivating students to learn, managing student behavior, grouping students for instruction, and testing and evaluating students. These functions are carried out at two levels. At the school level, the principal and/or central administrators may establish policies concerning grouping of students (e.g., tracking), provision and allocation of special education and remedial resources, and grading, evaluation, and promotion practices. At the classroom level, teachers control the grouping of students within the class, teaching techniques, classroom management methods, informal incentives, frequency and form of quizzes and tests, and so on. These elements of school and classroom organization are at least as important for student achievement as the quality of teachers' lessons.

A Model of Effective Instruction

Slavin (1984) proposed a model of effective instruction which focused on the *alterable* elements of Carroll's model (1963, 1989) "Model of School Learning." These are the elements that teachers and schools can directly change. The components of this model of alterable elements of effective instruction are as follows:

1. *Quality of Instruction*: The degree to which information or skills are presented so that students can easily learn them. Quality of instruction is largely a product of the quality of the curriculum and of the lesson presentation itself.

2. *Appropriate Levels of Instruction:* The degree to which the teacher makes sure that students are ready to learn a new lesson (that is, they have the necessary skills and knowledge to learn it), but have not already learned the lesson. In other words, the level of instruction is appropriate when a lesson is neither too difficult nor too easy for students.

3. *Incentive*: The degree to which the teacher makes sure that students are motivated to work on instructional tasks and to learn the material being presented.

4. *Time*: The degree to which students are given enough time to learn the material being taught.

The four elements of this QAIT (Quality, Appropriateness, Incentive, Time) model have one important characteristic: *All four* must be adequate for instruction to be effective. Again, effective instruction is not just good teaching. No matter how high the quality of instruction, students will not learn a lesson if they lack the necessary prior skills or information, if they lack the motivation, or if they lack the time they need to learn the lesson. On the other hand, if the quality of instruction is low, then it makes no difference how much students know, how motivated they are, or how much time they have. Each of the elements of the QAIT model is like a link in a chain, and the chain is only as strong as its weakest link. In fact, it may be hypothesized that the four elements are *multiplicatively* related, in that improvements in multiple elements may produce substantially larger learning gains than improvements in any one.

Effective Classroom Organization

Most of the advances in recent research on teaching have come about as a result of correlational process-product research, in which the practices of instructionally effective teachers have been contrasted with those of less effective teachers, controlling for student inputs. In recent years, the findings of these process-product studies have been incorporated into coherent instructional programs and evaluated in field experiments. Other coherent instructional methods not based on the process-product findings, such as mastery learning, cooperative learning, tutoring, and individualized instruction methods, have also been evaluated in field experiments. Each of these instructional methods is based on its own psychological or educational theories. However, the QAIT model is meant to inform all potential forms of classroom organization. Given a relatively fixed set of resources, every innovation in classroom organization solves some problems but also creates new problems which must themselves be solved. Tradeoffs are always involved. Understanding the terms of these tradeoffs is critical for an understanding of how to build effective models of classroom organization.

The QAIT model is designed primarily to clarify the tradeoffs involved in alternative forms of classroom organization. This paper presents a perspective on what is known now about each of the QAIT elements and, more importantly, explores the theoretical and practical ramifications of the *interdependence* of these elements for effective school and classroom organization.

Quality of Instruction

Quality of instruction refers to the activities we think of first when we think of teaching: lecturing, discussing, calling on students, and so on. When instruction is high in quality, the information being presented makes sense to students, is interesting to them, is easy to remember and apply.

The most important aspect of instructional quality is the degree to which the lesson makes sense to students. For example, teachers must present information in an organized orderly way (Kallison 1986), note transitions to new topics (Smith and Cotton 1980), use clear and simple language (Land 1987), use many vivid images and examples (Hiebert, et al. 1991; Mayer and Gallini 1990), and frequently restate essential principles (Maddox and Hoole 1975). Lessons should be related to students' background knowledge, using such devices as advance organizers (Pressley, et al. 1992) or simply reminding students of previously learned material at relevant points in the lesson. Enthusiasm (Abrami, Leventhal, and Perry 1982) and humor (Kaplan and Pascoe 1977) can also contribute to quality of instruction, as can use of media and other visual representations of concepts (Hiebert, Wearne, and Taber 1991; Kozma 1991).

Clear specification of lesson objectives to students (Melton 1978) and a substantial correlation between what is taught and what is assessed (Cooley and Leinhardt 1980) contribute to instructional quality, as does frequent formal or informal assessment to see that students are mastering what is being taught (Crooks 1988; Kulik and Kulik 1988) and immediate feedback on the correctness of their performances (Barringer and Gholson 1979).

Instructional pace is partly an issue of quality of instruction and partly of appropriate levels of instruction. In general, content coverage is strongly related to student achievement (Dunkin 1978; Barr and Dreeben 1983), so a rapid pace of instruction may contribute to instructional quality. However, there is obviously such a thing as too rapid an instructional pace (see Leighton and Slavin 1988). Frequent assessment of student learning is critical for teachers to establish the most rapid instructional pace consistent with the preparedness and learning rate of all students.

Appropriate Levels of Instruction

Perhaps the most difficult problem of school and classroom organization is accommodating instruction to the needs of students with different levels of prior knowledge and different learning rates. If a teacher presents a lesson on long division to a heterogeneous class, some students may fail to learn it because they have not mastered such prerequisite skills as subtraction, multiplication, or simple division. At the same time, there may be some students who know how to divide before the lesson begins, or learn to do so very rapidly. If the teacher sets a pace of instruction appropriate to the needs of the students lacking prerequisite skills, then the rapid learners' time will be largely wasted. If the instructional pace is too rapid, the students lacking prerequisite skills will be left behind.

There are many common means of attempting to accommodate instruction to students' diverse needs, but each method has drawbacks that may make the method counterproductive. Various forms of ability grouping seek to reduce the heterogeneity of instructional groups. Special education and remedial programs are a special form of ability grouping designed to provide special resources to accelerate the achievement of students with learning problems. However, between-class ability grouping plans, such as tracking, can create low-ability classes for which teachers have low expectations and maintain a slow pace of instruction, and which many teachers dislike to teach (Good and Marshall 1984; Oakes 1985, 1987; Rowan and Miracle 1983; Slavin 1987b, 1990a). Similar problems make self-contained special education classes of questionable benefit to students with learning handicaps (see Leinhardt and Bickel 1987; Leinhardt and Pallay 1982; Madden and Slavin 1983). Within-class ability grouping, such as the use of reading and mathematics groups, creates problems of managing multiple groups within the classroom, reduces direct instruction to each student, and forces teachers to assign large amounts of unsupervised seatwork to keep students engaged while the teacher is working with a reading or mathematics group (Barr 1992).

Research on assignment of students to ability-grouped classes finds no achievement benefits for this practice at the elementary or secondary levels (see Slavin 1987b, 1990a; Oakes 1985, 1987). However, forms of ability grouping in which elementary students remain in heterogeneous classes most of the day but are regrouped into homogeneous reading or mathematics classes can be instructionally effective if teachers actually adapt their level and pace of instruction to meet the needs of the regrouped classes. In particular, the Joplin Plan, and certain nongraded plans in which elementary students are regrouped for reading or mathematics across grade lines and instructional level, is based on performance level rather than age can be instructionally effective (Slavin 1987b; Gutiérrez and Slavin 1992). Also, research on within-class ability grouping finds this practice to increase student mathematics achievement, particularly when the number of groups used is small and management techniques designed to ensure smooth transitions and high time-on-task during seatwork are used (Slavin 1987b; Slavin and Karweit 1984).

Group-based mastery learning (Bloom 1976; Block and Burns 1976; Guskey and Gates 1985) is an approach to providing levels of instruction that does not use permanent ability groups but rather regroups students after each skill is taught on the basis of their mastery of that skill. Students who attain pre-set criteria (e.g., 80%) on a formative test work on enrichment studies while non-masters receive corrective instruction. In theory, mastery learning should provide appropriate levels of instruction by ensuring that students have mastered prerequisite skills before they receive instruction in subsequent skills. However, within the confines of traditional class periods, the time needed for corrective instruction may slow the pace of instruction for the class as a whole. Studies of group-based mastery learning conducted in elementary and secondary schools over periods of at least four weeks have found few benefits of this approach in comparison to control groups given the same objectives, materials, and time as the mastery learning groups (Slavin 1987c).

The most extreme form of accommodation to individual differences short of one-to-one tutoring is individualized instruction, in which students work entirely at their own level and rate. Individualized instruction certainly solves the problem of providing appropriate levels of instruction, but it creates serious problems of classroom management, often depriving students of adequate direct instruction. Research on individualized instruction has not generally found positive effects on student achievement (Hartley 1977; Horak 1981). However, Team Assisted Individualization, a form of individualized instruction which also incorporates the use of cooperative learning groups, has been found to consistently increase student achievement in mathematics (Slavin, Leavey and Madden 1984; Slavin, Madden, and Leavey 1984; Slavin and Karweit 1985; Slavin 1985).

Incentive

Thomas Edison once wrote that "genius is one percent inspiration and ninety-nine percent perspiration." The same could probably be said for learning. Learning is work. This is not to say that learning must be drudgery, but it is certainly the case that students must exert themselves to pay attention, to study, and to conscientiously perform the tasks assigned to them, and they must somehow be motivated to do these things. This motivation may come from the intrinsic interest value of the material being learned, or may be created through the use of extrinsic incentives, such as praise, grades, stars, and so on (see Stipek 1993).

If students want to know something, they will be more likely to exert the necessary effort to learn it. This is why there are students who can rattle off the names and statistics relating to every player on their favorite sports team, but do not know their multiplication facts. Teachers can create intrinsic interest in material to be taught by arousing student curiosity, for example by using surprising demonstrations, by relating topics to students' personal lives, or by allowing students to discover information for themselves (Brophy 1987; Malone and Lepper 1988).

However, not every subject can be made intrinsically interesting to every student at all times. Most students need some sort of extrinsic incentive to exert an adequate level of effort on most school tasks. For example, studies of graded versus pass-fail college courses find substantially higher achievement in classes that give grades (Gold, Reilly, Silberman, and Lehr 1971; Hales, Bain, and Rand 1971). At the elementary level, informal incentives, such as praise and feedback, may be more important than the formal grading system (see Brophy 1987). One critical principle of effective use of classroom incentives is that students should be held accountable for everything they do. For example, homework that is checked has been found to contribute more to student achievement than homework that is assigned but not checked (Cooper 1989). Also, questioning strategies that communicate high expectations for students, such as waiting for them to respond (Rowe 1974) and following up with students who do not initially give full responses (Brophy and Evertson 1974), have been found to be associated with high achievement (see Good 1987).

Several methods of providing formal incentives for learning have been found to be instructionally effective. One practical and effective method of rewarding students for appropriate, learning-oriented behavior is home-based reinforcement (Barth 1979) through provision of daily or weekly reports to parents on student behavior. Another is group contingencies (Dolan, et al. 1992; Hayes 1976), in which the entire class or groups within the class are rewarded on the basis of the behavior of the entire group.

Cooperative learning methods (Slavin 1990b) involve students working in small learning groups to master academic material. Forms of cooperative learning that have consistently increased student achievement have provided rewards to heterogeneous groups based on the learning of their members. This incentive system motivates students to encourage and help one another to achieve. Rewarding students based on improvement over their own past performance has also been found to be an effective incentive system (Natriello 1987; Slavin 1980).

In addition to being a product of specific strategies designed to increase student motivation, incentive is also influenced by quality of instruction and appropriate levels of instruction. Students will be more motivated to learn about a topic that is presented in an interesting way, that makes sense to them, that they feel capable of learning. Further, a student's motivation to exert maximum effort will be influenced by their perception of the difference between their probability of success if they do exert themselves and their probability of success if they do not (Atkinson and Birch 1978; Slavin 1977, 1994). That is, if a student feels sure of success or, alternatively, of failure, regardless of his or her efforts, then incentive will be very low. This is likely to be the case if a lesson is presented at a level much too easy or too difficult for the student. Incentive is high when the level of instruction is appropriate for a student, so that the student perceives that with effort the material can be mastered, so that the payoff for effort is perceived to be great.

Time

Instruction takes time. More time spent teaching a subject does not always translate into additional learning, but if instructional quality, appropriateness of instruction, and incentives for learning are all high, then more time on instruction is likely to pay off in greater learning.

The amount of time available for learning depends largely on two factors: *Allocated time* and *engaged time*. Allocated time is the time scheduled by the teacher for a particular lesson or subject and then actually used for instructional activities. Allocated time is mostly under the direct control of the school and teacher. In contrast, engaged time, the time students actually engage in learning tasks, is not under the direct control of the school or the teacher. Engaged time, or time-on-task, is largely a product of quality of instruction, student motivation, and allocated time. Thus, allocated time is an alterable element of instruction (like quality, appropriateness, and incentive), but engaged time is a mediating variable linking alterable variables with student achievement.

While allocated time must be an essential element in any model of classroom organization, research on this variable has found few consistent effects on student achievement. For example, research on hours in the school day and days in the school year has found few relationships between these time variables and student achievement (Frederick and Walberg 1980; Karweit 1989). The Beginning Teacher Evaluation Study found that allocated time in specific subjects had no effect on student achievement in those subjects when time was measured at the class level (Marliave, Fisher, and Dishaw 1978). On the other hand, research on engaged time generally finds positive relationships between the time students are on task and their achievement, but even with this variable, results are inconsistent (see Karweit 1989).

Studies of means of increasing student time on task generally go under the heading of classroom management research. Process-product studies (see, for example, Brophy and Good 1986) have established that teachers' use of effective management strategies is associated with high student achievement. However, several experimental studies focusing on increasing time on-task have found that it is possible to increase engaged time and still have no significant effect on student achievement (Slavin 1986; Stallings and Krasavage 1986; Wilson and Nachtigal 1986).

Relating Alterable Elements of Instruction to Student Achievement

The QAIT model, whose elements were described in the previous sections, can also be conceptualized in terms of intermediate effects on time-related variables. Figure 1 depicts a model of how alterable elements of instruction might affect student achievement.

In Figure 1, two types of independent variables are presented: *Student inputs* and *alterable variables*. Student inputs refer to factors over which the school has little control in the short run: Student ability and those aspects of motivation to learn that students bring from home (as distinct from the motivation created by classroom practices). The alterable variables are the QAIT elements discussed earlier. Of course, student inputs are not immutable, but can be affected by classroom practices. For example, student aptitude to learn a specific lesson may be strongly influenced by background knowledge resulting from earlier instruction, by specific training in thinking, problem solving, or study skills, or by general intellectual stimulation or learning skills provided by the school. Student motivation to learn is also largely a product of past experiences in school. However, in the context of any given lesson, the student inputs can be considered fixed, while the alterable variables can be directly manipulated by the school or teacher.

The effects of the alterable variables on student achievement are held to be mediated by two time-related variables: *Instructional efficiency* and *engaged time*, or time-on-task. Instructional efficiency can be conceptualized as the amount of learning per time. For example, students will learn more in a ten-minute lesson high in instructional efficiency than in a lesson of similar length low in instructional efficiency. Engaged time is the amount of time students are actually participating in relevant learning activities, such as paying attention to lectures and doing assignments. Instructional efficiency is simply the inverse of Carroll's "time needed to learn," and engaged time is essentially his "time available for learning." Instructional efficiency and engaged time

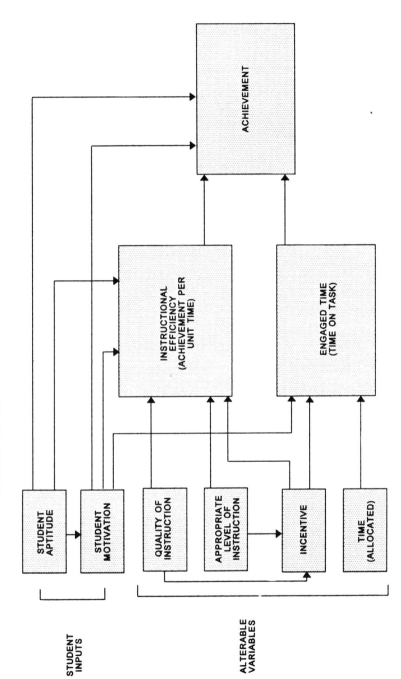

FIGURE 1

MODEL RELATING ALTERABLE ELEMENTS OF
INSTRUCTION TO STUDENT ACHIEVEMENT

Source: Slavin 1987a.

17

are multiplicatively related to student achievement; obviously, if either is zero, then learning is zero.

The QAIT model can be easily related to instructional efficiency and engaged time. Instructional efficiency is a product of the quality of instruction (e.g., organization and presentation quality of the lesson), appropriate levels of instruction (students have prerequisite skills but have not already learned the lesson), and incentive (students are interested in learning the lesson). Of course, aptitude and motivation also contribute to instructional efficiency for any given student. Engaged time is primarily a product of allocated time and incentive.

The relationship between improvements in each of the four alterable elements and effects on student achievement is held to be multiplicative. If any of the elements is at zero, learning will be zero. Above zero, the argument that the effects of the four elements are multiplicative rests in part on an assumption that effects of increasing each element are greatest at low levels and ultimately reach maximum or asymptotal levels (within a fixed amount of allocated time). For example, motivation to learn will reach a maximum in terms of affecting student achievement at some point. Effects of quality and appropriateness of instruction are similarly likely to reach a point of diminishing returns. Time on-task not only cannot be increased beyond 100% of time allocated, but it is doubtful whether increases beyond, say, 90% produce significant increases in learning. This may explain why several studies which produced substantial gains in time on-task have produced minimal effects on student achievement (see Emmer and Aussiker 1990; Slavin 1986).

The substantive implication of a multiplicative relationship among the QAIT elements is that it may be more effective to design instruction to produce moderate gains in two or more elements than maximize gains in only one. To increase a plant's growth, moderate increases in light, water, and fertilizer are likely to be more productive than large increases in only one of these elements. By the same token, substantial increases in any one element of the QAIT model, leaving all others unaffected, is likely to be less effective than more moderate, across-the-board improvements.

Another implication of the assumption that there is a point of diminishing returns in the achievement effect of each of the QAIT elements is that different types of programs will work differently in different settings depending on pre-existing levels of each. For example, a program focused on increasing time on-task is likely to be more effective in classrooms low on this variable than in those beginning at 80-90% levels. Highly motivated students may profit more from programs focusing on providing appropriate levels of instruction than from motivationally focused programs, and so on. Put another way, the relationship between each QAIT element and achievement is multiplicative, but the multiplier associated with improvements depends on where students began on each element. If, for example, quality of instruction is high but the level of instruction is inappropriate for many students, then the multiplier for increasing quality will be lower than that for increasing appropriateness.

The contention that the relationships between the QAIT variables, instructional efficiency, engaged time, and student achievement are multiplicative is pivotal to the model proposed here. In addition to implying that achievement will be zero if any of the alterable variables are zero, it also implies that while improving any one of the variables is likely to increase achievement arithmetically (up to a point of diminishing returns), improving more than one is likely to increase achievement geometrically. Since there are many random or uncontrolled factors in student achievement, and since achievement in any particular skill is so much a function of prior knowledge, ability, and motivation, it may be that for any new program to have a measurable effect on student mean achievement, it *must* improve multiple elements of instruction and therefore have a geometric effect on learning.

Effective Schools

Effective teaching behaviors are critical to student achievement, but there are also key factors at the school level that also contribute to instructional effectiveness. There is a body of research on school effectiveness that has identified characteristics associated with outstanding achievement gains. Some of these are simply aggregations of the characteristics of effective teachers. For example, schools that have an orderly environment, high time on task, and frequent monitoring of student progress tend to produce higher achievement than other schools (Mortimore et al. 1988; Purkey and Smith 1983; Teddlie and Stringfield 1993). However, there are also many elements of effective schooling that go beyond what happens in individual classrooms. For example, more effective schools are ones that have a clear academic mission and focus. They have principals who are strong instructional leaders, are proactive initiators of change, and encourage participation of the whole staff in making change (Teddlie and Stringfield 1993).

Effective Programs

Improvement in student achievement rarely comes about as a result of teachers and principals reading lists of effective teacher behaviors or school characteristics. On the contrary, effective school change usually comes about because schools and teachers adopt specific programs and practices that provide well validated teacher and student materials, staff development procedures, assessments, and so on (Slavin 1990c).

There are hundreds of well developed, replicable programs designed for specific subjects and grade levels (such as elementary math or high school biology). A listing of more than five hundred such programs is found in *Educational Programs that Work* (1987), a publication of the National Diffusion Network (NDN). The NDN is a program of the U.S. Department of Education designed to identify and help disseminate promising and replicable programs. The NDN programs are supposed to have evidence of effectiveness, and while the quality of evidence typically presented is often poor (see Klein 1992), there is at least some reason to believe that the programs are effective, and each is backed up by manuals, materials, and training services that make them relatively easy to replicate.

A few types of programs have particularly impressive evidence of effectiveness. One is cooperative learning methods, in which students work in small groups to help each other master academic material (Slavin 1990b). Cooperative methods incorporating group goals and individual accountability have been consistently more effective than traditional methods. Another is writing process methods (Hillocks 1984), in which students work in small groups to help one another develop as writers. Both cooperative learning and writing process methods have been used at all grade levels. Research has also supported the use of one-to-one tutoring for first graders who are at risk for school failure (Wasik and Slavin 1993). In particular, a program called Reading Recovery (Pinnell 1989) has been well researched and is widely used in the U.S. and elsewhere.

Recently, there has been a substantial focus in the U.S. on comprehensive school change programs. The most thoroughly evaluated and effective of these is a program called Success for All (Slavin et al. 1992, in press; Madden et al. 1993), a comprehensive restructuring of elementary schools to ensure that all children are successful from the early grades onward. Success for All uses research-based curriculum and instruction from prekindergarten to sixth grade, with an emphasis on cooperative learning. First graders who are at risk of reading failure may receive one-to-one tutoring by specially trained tutors. A comprehensive family support program builds positive relationships with parents and deals with such problems as truancy, vision and hearing problems, and behavior problems. Success for All may be particularly appropriate for Latin America because a version of its reading program exists in Spanish. The School Development Program (Comer 1988) is another comprehensive school change model that focuses primarily on building strong links between parents and schools.

A Strategy for Change

The most important lesson of research on effective teaching, effective schools, and effective programs is that to make a substantial difference in student achievement, change must be comprehensive and broad-based and must affect what teachers do with their children on a day-to-day basis. Reforms that have attempted to intervene in only one aspect of curriculum, instruction, or school organization are rarely as effective as those that deal with many critical elements at once. The Success for All program demonstrates the extreme case of this principle; Success for All affects every aspect of elementary education, and this model has been considerably more effective than programs affecting only one aspect of instruction or school organization.

Change in fundamental school practices is not easy or quick. Effective change strategies must include extensive inservice, followup, and internal assessment. It must incorporate effective materials and have adequate resources and infrastructure.

The unit of change is the school and classroom; changes above this level may support local changes but do not guarantee improved outcomes. Change must take place one school at a time, yet national or regional policies can create the conditions under which school-by-school change can be promoted and maintained.

School Improvement in Latin America

The situation of education in Latin America is highly diverse, both within and between Latin American nations. The prospects for effective changes are obviously quite different in schools with adequate basic resources and well-trained teachers than in schools lacking rudimentary facilities and qualified staff. Yet a few principles derived from research in the U.S. may apply.

First, the school must be the primary unit of change. Change will be most effective and cost-effective to the degree that it gives the professionals already in the schools effective programs and tools to do a better job. This implies a substantial investment in top-quality inservice. Preservice teacher training programs are important, of course, but schools must also have the capacity to train new staff members in the effective methods used in the school.

Second, change must be comprehensive. Change strategies must affect many aspects of instruction and school organization at once in order to magnify the effects.

Third, a continuing process of change must be set in motion. For example, school systems might introduce several proven or promising programs among a relatively small set of schools with a long-term plan of piloting, assessment, and expansion. A change process must start small and, once success is established, expand rapidly. Starting on too broad a scale risks failure from the outset.

Finally, the change process must respect local professionals and local conditions. No program, no matter how effective, will work in the same way everywhere. School staffs must have an opportunity to review possible programs and vote to adopt them and then to adapt them to their own local needs and resources.

This is an exciting time for educational reform throughout the world. Research is increasingly identifying replicable strategies for improving student achievement and other outcomes, and identifying means of introducing these strategies to schools. This paper has discussed some of the principles and practices of effective instruction and school organization with an eye toward informing policy makers concerned with improving schooling in Latin America, but the same basic principles would apply anywhere there is a commitment to educational reform.

BIBLIOGRAPHY

Abrami, P. C., L. Leventhal, and R. P. Perry. 1982. "Educational Seduction." *Review of Educational Research* 52: 446-462.

Anderson, L. M., N. L. Brubaker, J. Alleman-Brooks, and G. G. Duffy. 1985. "A Qualitative Study of Seatwork in First-grade Classrooms." *Elementary School Journal* 86: 123-140.

Anderson, L. M., C. Evertson, and J. Brophy. 1979. "An Experimental Study of Effective Teaching in First-Grade Reading-Groups." *Elementary School Journal* 79: 193-223.

Atkinson, J. W., and D. Birch. 1978. *Introduction to Motivation.* 2nd ed. New York: Van Nostrand.

Barr, R. 1992. "Teachers, Materials, and Group Composition in Literacy Instruction." *Elementary School Literacy: Critical Issues.* Eds. M. J. Dreher and W. H. Slater. Norwood, MA: Christopher-Gordon.

Barr, R., and R. Dreeben. 1983. *How Schools Work.* Chicago: University of Chicago Press.

Barringer, C., and B. Gholson. 1979. "Effects of Type and Combination of Feedback Upon Conceptual Learning by Children: Implications for Research in Academic Learning." *Review of Educational Research* 49: 459-478.

Barth, R. 1979. "Home-Based Reinforcement of School Behavior: A Review and Analysis." *Review of Educational Research* 49: 436-458.

Block, J. H., and R. B. Burns. 1976. "Mastery Learning." *Review of Research in Education (Vol. 4)*. Ed. L. S. Shulman. Itasca, IL: F. E. Peacock.

Bloom, B. S. 1976. *Human Characteristics and School Learning*. New York: McGraw-Hill.

Brophy, J. E. 1979. "Teacher Behavior and Its Effects." *Journal of Educational Psychology* 71: 733-750.

_____. 1981. "Teacher Praise: A Functional Analysis." *Review of Educational Research* 51: 5-32.

_____. 1987. "Synthesis of Research on Strategies for Motivating Students to Learn." *Educational Leadership* 45: 40-48.

Brophy, J. E., and C. M. Everston. 1974. *Process-Product Correlations in the Texas Teacher Effectiveness Study: Final Report* (Research Report No. 74-4). Austin: Research and Development Center for Teacher Education, University of Texas.

Brophy, J. E., and T. L. Good. 1986. "Teacher Behavior and Student Achievement." *Handbook of Research on Teaching*. Ed. M. C. Wittrock. 3rd ed. New York: McMillan.

Carroll, J. B. 1963. "A Model of School Learning." *Teachers College Record* 64: 723-733.

_____. 1989. "The Carroll Model: A 25-Year Retrospective and Prospective View." *Educational Research* 18: 26-31.

Cavanaugh, B. R. 1984. *Effects of Interdependent Group Contingencies on the Achievement of Elementary School Children*. Unpublished doctoral dissertation, University of Maryland.

Clark, C. M. 1987. "The Carroll Model." *International Encyclopedia of Teaching and Teacher Education*. Ed. M. J. Dunkin. New York: Pergamon.

Comer, J. 1988. "Educating Poor Minority Children." *Scientific American* 259: 42-48.

Cooley, W. W., and G. Leinhardt. 1980. "The Instructural Dimensions Study." *Educational Evaluation and Policy Analysis* 2: 7-35.

Cooper, H. 1989. "Synthesis of Research on Homework." *Educational Leadership* 47.3: 85-91.

Crooks, T. J. 1988. "The Impact of Classroom Evaluation Practices on Students." *Review of Educational Research* 58: 438-481.

Dolan, L. J., S. G. Kellam, C. H. Brown, L. Werthamer-Larsson, G. W. Rebok, L. S. Mayer, J. Laudolff, J. S. Turkkan, C. Ford, and L. Wheeler. 1992. "The Short-Term Impact of Two Classroom-Based Preventive Interventions on Aggressive and Shy Behaviors and Poor Achievement." *Journal of Applied Developmental Psychology* 14: 317-345.

Dunkin, M. 1978. "Student Characteristics, Classroom Processes, and Student Achievement." *Journal of Educational Psychology* 70: 998-1009.

Emmer, E. T., and A. Aussiker. 1990. "School and Classroom Discipline Programs: How Well Do They Work?" *Student Discipline Strategies*. Ed. O. C. Moles. Albany: State University of New York Press.

Evertson, C. M., J. K. Folger, C. Breda, and C. Randolph. 1990. "How Does Inservice Training Affect Teachers' Instruction in Small, Regular, and Regular/Aide Classes?" Paper presented at the annual convention of the American Educational Research Association, Boston.

Frederick, W., and H. Walberg. 1980. "Learning as a Function of Time." *Journal of Educational Research* 73: 183-194.

Gold, R. M., A. Reilly, R. Silberman, and R. Lehr. 1971. "Academic Achievement Declines Under Pass-Fail Grading." *Journal of Experimental Education* 39: 17-21.

Good, T. 1987. "Teacher Expectations." *Talks to Teachers*. Eds. D. Berliner and B. Rosenshine. New York: Random House. 159-200.

Good, T., and S. Marshall. 1984. "Do Students Learn More in Heterogeneous or Homogenous Groups?" *The Social Context of Instruction: Group Organization and Group Processes*. Eds. P. Peterson, L. C. Wilkinson, and M. Hallihan. New York: Academic Press. 15-38.

Guskey, T. R., and S. L. Gates. 1985. "A Synthesis of Research on Group-Based Mastery Learning Programs." Paper presented at the annual convention of the American Educational Research Association, Chicago.

Gutiérrez, R., and R. E. Slavin. 1992. "Achievement Effects of the Nongraded Elementary School: A Best-Evidence Synthesis." *Review of Educational Research* 62: 333-376.

Hales, L. W., P. T. Bain, and L. P. Rand. 1971. "An Investigation of Some Aspects of the Pass-Fail Grading System." Paper presented at the annual meeting of the American Educational Research Association, New York.

Hartley, S. S. 1977. "Meta-Analysis of the Effects of Individually Paced Instruction in Mathematics." *Dissertation Abstracts International* 38: 4003A. (University Microfilms No. 77-29, 926).

Hayes, L. 1976. "The Use of Group Contingencies for Behavioral Control: A Review." *Psychological Bulletin* 83: 628-648.

Hiebert, J., D. Wearne, and S. Taber. 1991. "Fourth Graders' Gradual Construction of Decimal Fractions During Instruction Using Different Physical Representations." *Elementary School Journal* 91: 321-341.

Hillocks, G. 1984. "What Works in Teaching Composition: A Meta-Analysis of Experimental Treatment Studies." *American Journal of Education* 93: 133-170.

Horak, V. M. 1981. "A Meta-Analysis of Research Findings on Individualized Instruction in Mathematics." *Journal of Educational Research* 74: 249-253.

Kallison, J. M. 1986. "Effects of Lesson Organization on Achievement." *American Educational Research Journal* 23: 337-347.

Kaplan, R. M., and G. C. Pascoe. 1977. "Humorous Lectures and Humorous Examples: Some Effects Upon Comprehension and Retention." *Journal of Educational Psychology* 69: 61-65.

Karweit, N. L. 1989. "Time and Learning: A Review." *School and Classroom Organization.* Ed. R. E. Slavin. Hillsdale, NJ: Erlbaum.

Klein, S. S. 1992. "A Framework for Redesigning an R and D-Based National Education Dissemination System in the United States." *Knowledge: Creation, Diffusion, Utilization* 13.3: 256-286.

Kozma, R. 1991. "Learning With Media." *Review of Educational Research* 61.2: 179-211.

Kulik, J. A., and C. L. Kulik. 1988. "Timing of Feedback and Verbal Learning." *Review of Educational Research* 58: 79-97.

Land, M. L. 1987. "Vagueness and Clarity." *International Encyclopedia of Teaching and Teacher Education.* Ed. M. J. Dunkin. New York: Pergamon.

Leighton, M. S., and R. E. Slavin. 1988. "Achievement Effects of Instructional Pace and Systematic Instruction in Elementary Mathematics." Paper presented at the annual convention of the American Educational Research Association, New Orleans.

Leinhardt, G., and W. Bickel. 1987. "Instruction's the Thing Wherein to Catch the Mind That Falls Behind." *Educational Psychologist* 22: 177-207.

Leinhardt, G., and A. Pallay. 1982. "Restrictive Educational Settings: Exile or Haven?" *Review of Educational Research* 52: 557-578.

Madden, N. A., and R. E. Slavin. 1983. "Mainstreaming Students With Mild Academic Handicaps: Academic and Social Outcomes." *Review of Educational Research* 84: 131-138.

Madden, N. A., R. E. Slavin, N. L. Karweit, L. J. Dolan, and B. A. Wasik. 1993. "Success for All: Longitudinal Effects of a Restructuring Program for Inner-City Elementary Schools." *American Educational Research Journal* 30: 123-148.

Maddox, H., and E. Hoole. 1975. "Performance Decrement in the Lecture." *Educational Review* 28: 17-30.

Malone, T., and M. Lepper. 1988. "Making Learning Fun: A Taxonomy of Intrinsic Motivation for Learning." *Aptitude Learning and Instruction, Vol. III: Cognitive and Affective Process Analysis.* Eds. R. Snow and M. Farr. Hillsdale, NJ: Erlbaum.

Marliave, R., C. Fisher, and M. Dishaw. 1978. *Academic Learning Time and Student Achievement in the B-C Period.* Far West Laboratory for Educational Research and Development. Technical Note V-29.

Mayer, R. E., and J. K. Gallini. 1990. "When Is an Illustration Worth Ten Thousand Words?" *Journal of Educational Psychology* 82: 715-726.

Melton, R. F. 1978. "Resolution of Conflicting Claims Concerning the Effect of Behavioral Objectives on Student Learning." *Review of Educational Research* 48: 291-302.

Mortimore, P., P. Sammons, L. Stoll, D. Lewis, and R. Scob. 1988. *School Matters: The Junior Years*. Somerset, England: Open Books.

National Diffusion Network. 1987. *Educational Programs That Work*. 13th ed. Longmont, CO: Sopris West.

Natriello, G. 1987. "The Impact of Evaluation Processes on Students." *Educational Psychologist* 22: 155-175.

Oakes, J. 1985. *Keeping Track: How Schools Structure Inequality*. New Haven, CT: Yale University Press.

_____. 1987. "Tracking in Secondary Schools: A Contextual Perspective." *Educational Psychologist* 22: 129-153.

Pinnell, G. S. 1989. "Reading Recovery: Helping At-Risk Children Learn to Read." *Elementary School Journal* 90: 161-182.

Pressley, M., E. Wood, V. E. Woloshyn, V. Martin, A. King, and D. Menke. 1992. "Encouraging Mindful Use of Prior Knowledge: Attempting to Construct Explanatory Answers Facilitates Learning." *Educational Psychologist* 27: 91-109.

Purkey, S. C., and M. S. Smith. 1983. "Effective Schools: A Review." *Elementary School Journal* 83: 427-452.

Rosenshine, B. V., and R. J. Stevens. 1986. "Teaching Functions." *Third Handbook of Research on Teaching*. Ed. M. C. Wittrock. Chicago: Rand McNally.

Rowan, B., and A. Miracle. 1983. "Systems of Ability Grouping and the Stratification of Achievement in Elementary Schools." *Sociology of Education* 56: 133-144.

Rowe, M. B. 1974. "Wait-Time and Rewards as Instructional Variables, Their Influence on Language, Logic, and Fate Control: Part One-Wait-Time." *Journal of Research in Science Teaching* 11: 81-94.

Slavin, R. E. 1977. "A New Model of Classroom Motivation." Paper presented at the annual convention of the American Educational Research Association, New York.

_____. 1980. "Effects of Individual Learning Expectations on Student Achievement." *Journal of Educational Psychology* 72: 520-524.

_____. 1983a. *Cooperative Learning*. New York: Longman.

_____. 1983b. "When Does Cooperative Learning Increase Student Achievement?" *Psychological Bulletin* 94: 429-445.

_____. 1984. "Component Building: A Strategy for Research-Based Instructional Improvement." *Elementary School Journal* 84: 255-269.

_____. 1985. "Team-Assisted Individualization: Combining Cooperative Learning and Individualized Instruction in Mathematics." *Learning to Cooperate,*

Cooperating to Learn. Eds. R. E. Slavin, S. Sharan, R. Hertz-Lazarowitz, C. Webb, and R. Schmuck. New York: Plenum. 177-209.

_____. 1986. "The Napa Evaluation of Madeline Hunter's ITIP: Lessons Learned." *Elementary School Journal* 87: 165-171.

_____. 1987a. "A Theory of School and Classroom Organization." *Educational Psychologist* 22: 89-108.

_____. 1987b. "Ability Grouping and Student Achievement in Elementary Schools: A Best-Evidence Synthesis." *Review of Educational Research* 57: 347-350.

_____. 1987c. "Mastery Learning Reconsidered." *Review of Educational Research* 57: 175-213.

_____. 1989. "Achievement Effects of Substantial Reductions in Class Size." *School and Classroom Organization.* Ed. R. E. Slavin. Hillsdale, NJ: Erlbaum. 247-257.

_____. 1990a. "Achievement Effects of Ability Grouping in Secondary Schools: A Best Evidence Synthesis." *Review of Educational Research* 60.3: 471-499.

_____. 1990b. *Cooperative Learning: Theory, Research and Practice.* Englewood Cliffs, NJ: Prentice-Hall.

_____. 1990c. "On Making a Difference." *Educational Researcher* 19.3: 30-34.

_____. 1994. *Educational Psychology: Theory into Practice.* 4th ed. Boston: Allyn and Bacon.

Slavin, R. E., and N. L. Karweit. 1985. "Effects of Whole-Class, Ability-Grouped, and Individualized Instruction on Mathematics Achievement." *American Educational Research Journal* 22: 351-367.

Slavin, R. E., M. Leavey, and N. A. Madden. 1984. "Combining Cooperative Learning and Individualized Instruction: Effects on Student Mathematics Achievement, Attitudes, and Behaviors." *Elementary School Journal* 84: 409-422.

Slavin, R. E., N. A. Madden, L. J. Dolan, B. A. Wasik, S. Ross, and L. Smith. In press. "Whenever and wherever we choose...: The repliation of Success for All." *Phi Delta Kappa.*

Slavin, R. E, N. A. Madden, N. L. Karweit, L. Dolan, and B. A. Wasik. 1992. *Success for All: A Relentless Approach to Prevention and Early Intervention in Elementary Schools.* Arlington, VA: Educational Research Service.

Slavin, R. E., N. A. Madden, and M. Leavey. 1984. "Effects of Team Assisted Individualization on the Mathematics Achievement of Academically Handicapped and Non-Handicapped Students." *Journal of Educational Psychology* 76: 813-819.

Smith, L. R., and M. L. Cotton. 1980. "Effect of Lesson Vagueness and Discontinuity on Student Achievement and Attitudes." *Journal of Educational Psychology* 72: 670-675.

Stallings, J. A., and D. Kaskowitz. 1974. *Follow-Through Classroom Observation Evaluation 1972-73*. Menlo Park, CA: Stanford Research Institute.

Stallings, J., and E. M. Krasavage. 1986. "Program Implementation and Student Achievement in a Four-Year Madeline Hunter Follow Through Project." *Elementary School Journal* 87: 117-138.

Stipek, D. J. 1993. *Motivation to Learn: From Theory to Practice*. 2nd ed. Boston: Allyn and Bacon.

Teddlie, C., and S. Stringfield. 1993. *Schools Make a Difference: On Lessons Learned From a 10-Year Study of School Effects*. New York: Teachers College Press.

Wasik, B. A., and R. E. Slavin. 1993. "Preventing Early Reading Failure With One-To-One Tutoring: A Review of Five Programs." *Reading Research Quarterly* 28: 178-200.

Wilson, R. R., and P. Nachtigal. 1986. *Final Report: Cotopaxi/Westcliffe Follow Through Project*. Office of Educational Research and Improvement, Grant No. 400-81-0039.

Word, E., J. Johnston, H. P. Bain, B. D. Fulton, J. B. Zaharias, M. N. Lintz, C. M. Achilles, J. Floger, and C. Breda. 1990. *Student/Teacher Achievement Ratio (STaR): Tennessee's k-3 Class Size Study, Final Report*. Nashville: Tennessee State Department of Education.

EDUCATION FINANCE IN LATIN AMERICA: PERILS AND OPPORTUNITIES

Fernando Reimers [*]

SUMMARY

The education systems of Latin America show poor results in terms of providing quality of education equitably. In part this is because the region spends less per student at all levels than most regions in the world. This gap in per pupil expenditures between Latin America and the world is growing.

Although relative to overall government expenditure, countries in Latin America spend as much in education as do other regions, relative to gross national product they spend less. This suggests that the underfinancing of the sector is a result of the low tax base rather than of low government priority to the education sector. The ratio of expenditures per students to per capita GNP between different levels is smaller in Latin America than in Africa and is similar to that in Asia. In Latin America a higher proportion of education budgets is spent in recurrent expenditures, and a higher share for higher education. The share of enrollments in the private sector is at the high end in Latin America, relative to other regions.

The paper concludes by proposing options for reform including, but not limited to, increasing the level of resources for education. Policy analysis capacity should be developed in Ministries of Education to utilize existing resources better. Resources should also be used to promote innovations to improve the mix of inputs and the technical efficiency of education.

---

[*]   Fernando M. Reimers is an Institute associate at the Harvard Institute for International Development, where he specializes in education policy analysis, research, and planning. He also teaches a graduate course on education policy in Latin America at the Harvard Graduate School of Education. He obtained his doctorate in educational planning at Harvard University and has published several books and articles on education finance and development in Latin America. He has been a consultant for the Inter-American Development Bank, the World Bank, USAID, and UNESCO.

Introduction

This paper examines the financing of public education in Latin America, and compares the patterns of financing in the region with those of other regions in the world. In conclusion, the paper proposes options to address the constraints identified in the analysis.

The analysis is based on original computations using data from UNESCO's *World Education Report 1991*. For comparative purposes countries were grouped in eight geographical regions: Sub-Saharan Africa, Other African countries, Latin America, U.S. and Canada, Other countries in the Americas (including the Caribbean, Belize, Suriname, Guyana), Asia, Europe and the former Soviet Republics and Oceania. Appendix 1 lists the countries which were included in each region.

The paper is structured in ten sections. The first section of the paper outlines the problem of low levels of performance of the education systems and links that problem to the theme of finance.

Section II examines the absolute levels of expenditure in education for primary, secondary and tertiary education for Latin America and other regions of the world. Section III analyzes the growing gap in education expenditures between Latin America and other regions. Section IV discusses the level of effort government makes to finance education, which leads to an analysis of the level of effort in education relative to national resources (section V), and to an examination of the effort to fund students at different levels (section VI). Section VII discusses the relative emphasis in each level of education, analyzing per pupil expenditure at each level relative to other levels. Section VIII reviews the distribution of education expenditures by type and level. Finally (section IX) the paper discusses the role of privately financed education at different levels. The last section of the paper discusses the findings of this study and proposes recommendations to address the major financial constraints in the context of the undergoing economic transformations in Latin America.

In each section I first examine how all countries in the world, for which data are available, perform on each indicator, and then examine the performance of Latin America relative to other regions. In addition, I also provide comparative evidence from countries in other regions, which have levels of per capita income that fall within the same range as the levels of income per capita in Latin America.[1]

I.   The Problem

Latin America has the doubtful distinction of being the region with the most inequitable income distribution in the world.[2] As leaders of the countries of the region recognize the need to systemically reduce inequities, increase competitiveness, consolidate democratic institutions and promote stability and accountability, they will increasingly have to turn to educational institutions.

A look at the education systems of Latin America, however, shows systems that are turning out products of dubious quality and at low efficiency. Children are completing the first four grades of primary school without basic reading and math skills. Secondary school graduates seem to have been better prepared to continue onto higher education than to find opportunities for productive employment. Graduates at the tertiary level abound in fields that are at some distance from the most productive or dynamic sectors of the economy. In sum, the education system at all levels seems to be doing a better job at providing credentials than at developing basic skills, entrepreneurial abilities, critical thinking, citizenship, talent or social responsibility.

A recent study of the International Association of Educational Achievement assessed the reading ability of children in school at ages 9 and 14. Using equivalent instruments students were tested in 32 countries. Venezuela was the only Latin American country included in the study.[3] The results show that Venezuelan students have one of the lowest levels of reading ability in the world. Fourth grade students have on average the lowest level of achievement of all 32 countries studied. In the section of the test measuring the ability to obtain information from tables or instructions, the average Venezuelan student has a lower ability than the 5% lowest performing students in Finland, Hong Kong or the United States, the countries with highest scores. The best 5% among the Venezuelan students have lower results on the test than the average student in Finland, Hong Kong or the United States. In grade 9, the performance of Venezuelan students is one of the four worst in the 32 countries, followed by Nigeria, Zimbabwe and Botswana.

A standardized test in mathematics and science administered to students in Brazil, China, England and Portugal shows that Brazilian students have the lowest scores. While Chinese students scored 80% of the answers in the math test correctly, students in Sao Paulo only scored 37%, and those in Fortaleza only 32%. In science Chinese students obtained 67% of the answers on the test correctly, but students in Sao Paulo scored only 53% and those in Fortaleza only 46%.[4]

The problem of low quality educational results is compounded as students progress through the system. A recent education assessment in Paraguay identified that many entrants to university had serious limitations in reading and writing ability.[5]

In addition to generating low levels of learning, schools also fail to reduce social inequities, as the opportunity to learn is smaller for rural and poor children. Data from Chile obtained administering a basic skills test to primary school students show that while students from families in the highest quintile of the income distribution answer 80% of the questions correctly, students in the lowest quintile answer only 40% of them correctly.[6] A test administered to 3,248 primary school students (in grade six) in a random sample of Mexican schools shows that on average they answered only 48% of the items correctly in a curriculum test of basic subjects.[7] Students in Mexican private schools obtain higher scores (65%) than their counterparts in public schools (47%).

There is little disagreement that the product of schools leaves much to be desired. A related problem is that schools turn out their product in very inefficient ways. Grade repetition (estimated at 40% for first grade and 30% for primary education, at a cost of almost 2 billion dollars per year)[8] is a serious constraint on the internal efficiency of the system and another sign of low quality.

The educational establishment also perpetuates, rather than help-ing reduce, the inequalities that characterize Latin American societies. Although most of the children of school age in the region are enrolled in primary school at some point in their lives, there are great disparities between and within countries in the region in how many children are left out of school. Furthermore, for those who are enrolled there are great disparities in the opportunity to learn for children from different socioeconomic backgrounds and for those living in urban and rural areas. As a result, although many enroll in primary school at some point in their lives, many enroll in schools that put them at such disadvan-tage—compounded by their own social disadvantage—that school fail-ure is the most probable outcome; many of these children learn little, repeat several times, and eventually drop out of school.

The children who do not have access to education are dis-proportionately children from poor and rural families. In Costa Rica, for instance, according to survey data from 1982, 13.3% of the children in the age group 7-12 with no schooling were from the lowest income quintile and only 2.6% from the two highest income groups.[9] In Bolivia, where only 80% of the six-year olds and 93% of the seven-year olds in the bottom quintile are enrolled in school, the corresponding figures for the highest quintile are 95% and 98% respectively. At age seven most children in the highest quintile are enrolled in school, while for the bottom quintile this only happens at age nine. While 94% of the 15-year olds in the highest quintile are still enrolled in school, for the bottom quintile enrollment drops below 90% after children reach 13 years of age. (Figures derived from Encuesta de Hogares 1990, Bolivia. This survey was administered in the major cities in Bolivia in 1990. Only households located in cities with more than 10,000 persons were included in the sample.)

Table 1 shows that in El Salvador, children from poor homes are less likely to enroll in school, do it later and stay fewer years in school than their wealthier counterparts. While in the poorest 20% of the population only one in every two children are enrolled in school by age seven, in the 10% wealthiest group nine out of ten children attend school at that age. For the poorest 20% of the population only three out of every four children attend school at age nine for three years, while for the wealthiest 10%, three out of four children attend school by age five, nine out of ten attend by age seven and until age 14.

TABLE 1

PERCENTAGE OF CHILDREN ENROLLED IN SCHOOL BY AGE
AND INCOME GROUP IN EL SALVADOR IN 1991

AGE	4	5	6	7	8	9	10	11	12	13	14	15
Poorest 20%	7	16	30	55	66	74	75	76	71	64	53	45
2nd Quintile	11	20	38	62	71	80	83	81	78	70	59	52
3rd Quintile	20	36	54	71	84	87	88	87	84	74	72	58
4th Quintile	30	53	74	84	91	93	94	95	91	86	74	70
9th Quintile	41	69	83	90	96	90	96	96	94	89	79	81
Richest 10%	53	74	85	91	99	95	96	97	92	90	87	82

Source: Derived from data obtained in the *Encuesta de Hogares de Propósitos Múltiples Urbano y Rural*. Ministerio de Planificación. El Salvador, 1991.

A related fact constraining access is the different quality of the services provided to children from different groups. With regard to public education, as with many other fields of State activity in Latin America, those who have more, get more.

It should not be surprising that proportionately more people in rural areas have no access to schooling since those are the areas least served by the State in providing education. Many of the schools in rural areas have teachers teaching more than one grade (a rare phenomenon in urban schools), and have teachers with less training, supervision and access to materials. Many of the rural schools also do not offer all grades of primary education. In 1987 in Colombia 23% of the urban teachers were untrained versus 39% of the rural teachers; in Honduras the figures were 15% versus 46%; in Nicaragua they were 32% versus 74%.[10]

In Peru the percentage of trained teachers (*maestros titulados*) in primary education ranges from 95% in Arequipa (where the reported repetition rate is 11%), or over 70% in Lima (repetition rates around 10%), down to 20% of trained teachers in Madre de Dios (repetition rate 46%).[11]

Table 2 shows that the percentage of public "incomplete schools" (not offering all grades) is much higher in rural than in urban areas.

TABLE 2

PERCENTAGE OF INCOMPLETE SCHOOLS IN
URBAN AND RURAL AREAS IN 1987

Country	Percentage Urban	Percentage Rural
Bolivia	0.0%	29.6%
Colombia	26.2%	62.1%
Ecuador	26.0%	88.6%
El Salvador	3.4%	62.8%
Panama	2.1%	11.3%

Source: UNESCO. OREALC. *Situación educativa de América Latina y el Caribe 1980-1987.* Santiago, Chile. 1990. 34.

Given these problems, what is the significance of educational finance? Education funds are necessary to pay for teachers' salaries, for the construction of schools, for teaching materials and other resources. The question of finance concerns how much should be spent to accomplish the task of teaching effectively, how resources should be allocated and who should pay.

The rest of this paper examines the patterns of response that the countries of Latin America have given to these three questions, and how those compare to the responses given by other regions. The paper concludes with a discussion of the significance of these patterns in the current context of the economic transformation being experienced by Latin America.

II. Latin America Invests Less Per Student
at All Levels than Most Regions in the World

Primary Education

For all countries of the world expenditures per pupil in primary school (in 1989) range from US$ 11 to US$ 8,400. On average countries for which I have data spend US$ 887. Half of the countries spend US$ 162.

TABLE 3

EXPENDITURES PER PRIMARY SCHOOL STUDENT
IN 1989 IN US$ PER REGION

	Mean	Std. Dev.	Countries
For All Countries	886.52	1593.45	98
Other Africa	101.20	69.62	3
Sub-Saharan Africa	81.13	92.49	28
Latin America	**116.93**	**81.68**	**14**
Caribbean and Other	601.69	596.00	8
US and Canada	3,896.10	138.73	2
Asia	548.69	869.77	19
Europe and USSR	2,622.17	2,377.25	21
Oceania	1,523.33	1,245.06	3
Countries within the same range of per capita GNP as Latin America			
Other Africa	132.30	62.37	2
Sub-Saharan Africa	103.40	64.65	12
Caribbean and Other	554.37	783.92	4
Asia	136.64	103.26	7
Europe and USSR	351.37	133.92	4
Oceania	109.20	.00	1

Source: UNESCO. *World Education Report*. Santiago, Chile. 1991.

Latin America spends, on average, less per primary school student than any other region, with the exception of Africa. As table 2 shows, Latin America spends one fifth per primary school student of what is spent by Asia or the Caribbean, and less than one twentieth of what is spent by Europe or the U.S. and Canada. Countries of comparable per capita income in Asia spend, on average, 20% more per primary school student than countries in Latin America. Countries of similar income levels in the Caribbean spend almost five times as much as Latin American countries.

Education spending per primary student in Latin America ranges from US$ 24 to US$ 255. On average, countries spend US$ 117; half of the countries spend less than US$ 96. Two in five countries in the world spend more than the highest spending country in Latin America at this level.

Secondary Education

Expenditures on secondary education range from US$ 19 per pupil to US$ 6,712. On average, countries spend US$ 1,013 per secondary school student. Half of the countries spend less than US$ 268.

Latin America also spends less, on average, per secondary school student than any other region in the world as seen in table 4. African countries spend twice as much per student at this level, the Caribbean spends three times as much, and Asia spends five times as much. Europe, the U.S. and Canada spend 19 and 34 times as much, respectively. Latin America spends less per secondary school student than countries in other regions of comparable levels of income per capita.

Spending on secondary school students in Latin America ranges from US$ 32 to US$ 376. On average, countries in the region spend US$ 167 in this level; half of the countries spend less than US$ 104 per student. Two in five countries in the world spend more than the highest-spending country in Latin America per secondary school student.

Higher Education

Expenditures per student in higher education range from US$ 33 to US$ 13,536. On average, countries spend US$ 3,079 per student at this level. Half of the countries for which I have data spend less than US$ 1,924.

At the tertiary level Latin America spends, on average, less per student than any other region in the world as seen in table 5. Countries in Sub-Saharan Africa spend three times as much per student at this level; countries in Asia spend four times as much. The U.S. and Canada spend 14 times as much at this level. Asian countries of comparable

TABLE 4

EXPENDITURES PER SECONDARY SCHOOL STUDENT
IN 1989 IN US$ PER REGION

	Mean	Std. Dev.	Countries
For All countries	1,013.40	1,581.33	84
Other Africa	284.85	220.83	2
Sub-Saharan Africa	320.08	518.91	26
Latin America	**167.18**	**120.04**	**13**
Caribbean and Other	504.10	349.95	8
US and Canada	5,697.00	.00	1
Asia	808.59	1,182.28	16
Europe and USSR	3,095.77	2,006.96	16
Oceania	930.50	1,187.23	2

Countries within the same range of per capita GNP as Latin America

	Mean	Std. Dev.	Countries
Other Africa	441.00	.00	1
Sub-Saharan Africa	301.01	189.45	10
Caribbean and Other	397.50	160.94	4
Asia	200.12	197.35	5
Europe and USSR	408.80	254.56	2
Oceania	91.00	.00	1

Source: UNESCO. *World Education Report.* Santiago, Chile. 1991.

income levels spend 50% more per student in higher education than countries in Latin America.

Spending per student in higher education in Latin America ranges from US$ 33 to US$ 1,709. On average, countries spend US$ 649; half of the countries spend less than US$ 457 per student at this level. Fifty-four percent of the countries in the world spend more than the highest spending country in Latin America.

III. The Gap Between Latin America and the World Is Growing

Between 1980 and 1988 education expenditures in real terms decreased in 28% of the countries. Changes in education expenditures ranged from decreases of 14.7% per year to 25% average annual increases. In half of the countries the increase was less than 2.9% per year. On average, expenditures grew 2.9% per year.

TABLE 5

**EXPENDITURES PER TERTIARY SCHOOL STUDENT
IN 1989 IN US$ PER REGION**

	Mean	Std. Dev.	Countries
For All Countries	3,078.89	3,365.1512	93
Other Africa	1,285.10	858.69	3
Sub-Saharan Africa	2,095.13	1,110.10	23
Latin America	**648.51**	**498.75**	**14**
Caribbean and Other	2,081.65	1,117.92	8
US and Canada	9,205.30	2,796.89	2
Asia	2,595.20	3,621.98	19
Europe and USSR	5,949.72	4,087.86	21
Oceania	5,299.27	4,071.31	3

Countries within the same range of per capita GNP as Latin America

	Mean	Std. Dev.	Countries
Other Africa	1,338.75	1,207.24	2
Sub-Saharan Africa	2,357.16	1,063.58	10
Caribbean and Other	2,246.55	1,554.82	4
Asia	984.29	1,110.48	7
Europe and USSR	1,271.35	371.49	4
Oceania	1,110.20	.00	1

Source: UNESCO. *World Education Report*. Santiago, Chile. 1991.

The rate of growth of educational expenditures in real terms during the 1980s was slower, on average, in Latin America than in any other region of the world. Education expenditures in real terms increased 3 times faster in Sub-Saharan Africa, 3 times faster in Europe and the former Soviet Republics, 5 times faster in the U.S. and Canada, and 11 times faster in Asia. These results are summarized in table 6.

IV. How Much Effort Do Governments in Latin America Make in Education?

As an indicator of government support for education, I examined the percentage of education expenditures relative to all public expenditures. This indicator suggests that the governments of Latin America make efforts that are comparable, in relative terms, to those of governments in other regions. This is paradoxical given the fact that we have

TABLE 6

**ANNUAL AVERAGE GROWTH (%) IN EDUCATIONAL
EXPENDITURES IN REAL TERMS 80-88**

	Mean	Std. Dev.	Countries
For All Countries	2.92%	5.20%	119
Other Africa	5.52%	3.91%	6
Sub-Saharan Africa	1.97%	5.99%	34
Latin America	**.62%**	**4.62%**	**19**
Caribbean and Other	1.46%	4.39%	8
US $ Canada	3.20%	.56%	2
Asia	6.87%	5.68%	24
Europe and USSR	2.05%	1.95%	22
Oceania	1.80%	.90%	4
Countries within the same range of per capita GNP as Latin America			
Other Africa	6.20%	.28%	4
Sub-Saharan Africa	2.88%	3.65%	10
Caribbean and Other	.90%	5.09%	2
Asia	3.52%	2.97%	8
Europe and USSR	2.67%	2.94%	3
Oceania	1.80%	1.55%	2

Source: UNESCO. *World Education Report.* Santiago, Chile. 1991.

seen how, in absolute terms, spending per pupil in Latin America is smaller than in any other region. This paradox is resolved in the following section which shows how education spending relative to GNP is lower for Latin America than for any other region. This suggests that the gap in education spending between Latin America and the world is a function of the low tax base in the region.

In 1988 education expenditures ranged from 4.7% of public expenditures to 27%. Half of the countries in the world spent less than 14.5% of the public budget on education; on average they spent 14.8%. Table 6 shows that Latin America is at the high end of education spending relative to public expenditures.

A pervasive problem in the region is the gap between allocated and executed budgets. For example, in 1991 the Ministry of Education of Guatemala spent only 83% of the allocated budget for recurrent expenditures, and only 49% of the budget for capital expenditures.[12] This reflects a common problem: the lack of financial expertise in the Ministries of Education that prevents fluid communication and negotiation with Ministries of Finance. As Ministries of Finance have implemented more mechanisms to discourage spending (as a response to the adjustment process), Ministries of Education have been unable to disburse the funds allocated to finance their activities (particularly funds which are not for salaries). This in turn reduces the prospects of negotiating larger budgets for these purposes in future years.

V. Is the Level of Effort Sufficient?

Even though the level of governments' relative commitment to education is similar in Latin America to that of other regions, education expenditures are substantially lower relative to per capita income because Latin American governments spend less than other regions relative to gross national product (GNP).

TABLE 7

EDUCATION EXPENDITURES AS A PERCENTAGE
OF GOVERNMENT EXPENDITURES IN 1988, BY REGION

	Mean	Std. Dev.	Countries
For All Countries	14.78%	5.24%	101
Other Africa	19.82%	6.34%	6
Sub-Saharan Africa	15.87%	5.66%	25
Latin America	**17.21%**	**3.73%**	**15**
Caribbean and Other	15.62%	5.36%	6
US and Canada	15.60%	.00%	1
Asia	13.32%	4.70%	24
Europe and USSR	11.08%	3.77%	20
Oceania	17.10%	3.64%	4

Source: UNESCO. *World Education Report*. Santiago, Chile. 1991.

In 1988 expenditures in education ranged from 1.4% of GNP to 10.1%. Half of the countries in the world spent 4.7% of their national product on education; on average they spent 4.9%.

In 1988, on average, Latin America spent less on education relative to GNP than any other region in the world, as seen in table 8. Countries in Latin America spend, on average, half of what their counterparts in the Caribbean, or the U.S. and Canada, spend in education relative to GNP. The same pattern is observed if we restrict the comparison to countries within the same range of per capita GNP.

TABLE 8

**EDUCATION EXPENDITURE AS A PERCENTAGE OF
GNP IN 1988 BY REGION OF THE WORLD**

	Mean	Std. Dev.	Countries
For All Countries	4.86%	1.96%	120
Other Africa	7.33%	2.21%	6
Sub-Saharan Africa	4.38%	1.89%	28
Latin America	**3.69%**	**1.54%**	**17**
Caribbean and Other	6.94%	1.67%	10
US and Canada	6.95%	.21%	2
Asia	4.13%	1.64%	26
Europe and USSR	5.23%	1.58%	27
Oceania	5.45%	.87%	4

Countries within the same range of per capita GNP as Latin America

Other Africa	7.17%	2.01%	4
Sub-Saharan Africa	4.95%	1.84%	9
Caribbean and Other	7.35%	.21%	2
Asia	4.08%	2.04%	7
Europe and USSR	5.05%	1.44%	4
Oceania	5.10%	1.27%	2

Source: UNESCO. *World Education Report*. Santiago, Chile. 1991.

One in three countries in Latin America is included in the lowest half—in terms of spending on education as a percentage of GNP—of all countries in the world. The exceptions are Cuba (6.7%), Honduras (4.8%), Nicaragua (6.2%) and Panama (5.6%). Eighteen percent of the countries in the world spend more than the highest spending country in Latin America (Cuba with 6.7%) and 20% of the countries spend more than the next highest spending country (Nicaragua with 6.2%).

41

VI. Relative Levels of Spending at Different Levels of Education

Latin America spends less per pupil relative to per capita income than any other region of the world at all levels.

In 1988 countries' per pupil spending in primary school ranged from 3% of per capita GNP to 91% of per capita GNP. Half the countries spent 12% or less of GNP per capita per primary school student. On average, countries spent 14% of per capita GNP per primary school student.

Expenditures per primary student relative to per capita GNP are lower in Latin America than in any other region in the world. Among countries within the same range of income per capita, Asian countries spend 19% more than Latin American countries, countries in Sub-Saharan Africa spend 63% more, and countries in the Caribbean spend 3.5 times more.

TABLE 9

EXPENDITURES PER PRIMARY SCHOOL STUDENT AS A PERCENTAGE OF PER CAPITA GNP IN 1988

	Mean	Std. Dev.	Countries
For All Countries	14%	10%	115
Other Africa	13%	2%	3
Sub-Saharan Africa	14%	8%	30
Latin America	**9%**	**4%**	**16**
Caribbean and Other	22%	23%	12
US and Canada	19%	2%	2
Asia	11%	3%	24
Europe and USSR	17%	8%	25
Oceania	15%	3%	3

Countries within the same range of per capita GNP as Latin America

	Mean	Std. Dev.	Countries
Other Africa	14%	0%	2
Sub-Saharan Africa	14%	7%	12
Caribbean and Other	30%	40%	4
Asia	10%	4%	7
Europe and USSR	15%	4%	4
Oceania	12%	0%	1

Source: UNESCO. *World Education Report*. Santiago, Chile. 1991.

In 1988 countries spent from 3% of per capita GNP to 1.7 times per capita GNP on every secondary school student. Half of the countries spent 22% or less of per capita GNP per secondary school student. On average, countries spend 30% of per capita GNP per secondary school student. Expenditure per pupil in secondary school relative to per capita GNP is lower in Latin America than in any other region of the world, including countries within the same range of per capita income, as seen in table 10.

TABLE 10

**EXPENDITURE PER SECONDARY SCHOOL STUDENT AS A
PERCENTAGE OF PER CAPITA GNP IN 1988**

	Mean	Std. Dev.	Countries
For All Countries	30%	30%	99
Other Africa	34%	1%	2
Sub-Saharan Africa	60%	44%	28
Latin America	**12%**	**7%**	**15**
Caribbean and Other	21%	7%	12
US and Canada	27%	0%	1
Asia	18%	8%	20
Europe and USSR	20%	6%	19
Oceania	12%	3%	2

Countries within the same range of per capita GNP as Latin America

	Mean	Std. Dev.	Countries
Other Africa	35%	0%	1
Sub-Saharan Africa	44%	25%	10
Caribbean and Other	24%	8%	4
Asia	13%	9%	5
Europe & USSR	18%	7%	2
Oceania	10%	0%	1

Source: UNESCO. *World Education Report*. Santiago, Chile. 1991.

In 1988 expenditures per university student ranged from 2% of per capita GNP to 16 times per capita GNP. Half of the countries spent 63% or more of per capita GNP per university student. On average, countries spend 1.8 times per capita GNP per university student.

Expenditures per university student relative to per capita GNP in Latin America are higher than in the U.S. and Europe as seen in table 11.

TABLE 11

EXPENDITURES PER STUDENT IN HIGHER EDUCATION AS A PERCENTAGE OF PER CAPITA GNP IN 1988

	Mean	Std. Dev.	Countries
For All Countries	186%	289%	108
Other Africa	184%	113%	3
Sub-Saharan Africa	575%	401%	24
Latin America	**52%**	**38%**	**16**
Caribbean and Other	142%	182%	11
US and Canada	46%	11%	2
Asia	76%	58%	24
Europe & USSR	46%	15%	25
Oceania	78%	39%	3
Countries within the same range of per capita GNP as Latin America			
Other Africa	125%	68%	2
Sub-Saharan Africa	344%	206%	10
Caribbean and Other	144%	97%	4
Asia	64%	49%	7
Europe and USSR	55%	11%	4
Oceania	122%	0%	1

Source: UNESCO. *World Education Report.* Santiago, Chile. 1991.

VII. Relations Between Per Pupil Expenditures at Different Levels

For countries of comparable per capita income, Latin America maintains a relative balance between expenditures in university students and in students in primary and secondary education, and between spending in secondary and primary school students. The gap between spending in these levels, by contrast, is much larger in Africa.

Most countries spend more resources per university student than per student in primary education. Countries range from those which spend 11% of expenditures per university student than per primary student (only four countries spend less for university students than primary students) to those who spend 123 times more per university student than per primary school student. Half of the countries spend six times or more per university student than per primary school student. On average, countries spend 15 times as much per university student as per primary school student.

On average, Latin America spends substantially less on university students (table 12) relative to primary school students than Africa and less than countries in the Caribbean. This ratio is slightly higher than that for Asia, but three and four times higher than the respective ratio in the U.S., Canada and Europe.

TABLE 12

AVERAGE EXPENDITURES PER PUPIL IN HIGHER EDUCATION RELATIVE TO EXPENDITURES PER PUPIL IN PRIMARY EDUCATION IN 1988 PER REGION

	Mean	Std. Dev.	Countries
For All Countries	15.21	23.46	108
Other Africa	16.04	12.74	3
Sub-Saharan Africa	46.05	33.28	24
Latin America	**6.31**	**4.18**	**16**
Caribbean and Other	9.29	10.29	11
US & Canada	2.38	.80	2
Asia	7.70	8.40	24
Europe and USSR	3.22	2.08	25
Oceania	5.56	4.02	3

Countries within the same range of per capita GNP as Latin America

	Mean	Std. Dev.	Countries
Other Africa	8.96	4.90	2
Sub-Saharan Africa	26.38	16.53	10
Caribbean and Other	13.79	10.77	4
Asia	5.87	3.20	7
Europe & USSR	4.04	1.67	4
Oceania	10.17	.00	1

Source: UNESCO. *World Education Report.* Santiago, Chile. 1991.

Most countries also spend more on each university student than on each secondary school student (only four countries spend more on secondary school students than on university students). Countries range from those who spend 10% of what they spend on each secondary school student on university students, to those who spend 25 times more on each secondary school student than on each university student. Half of the countries spend at least four times as much on university students as on secondary school students. On average, countries spend six times as much on university students as on secondary school students.

Latin American countries spend, on average, five times as much on university students than on students in secondary school. This is smaller than the respective ratios in Africa and the Caribbean and almost the same as the relative figure in Asia. Expenditures on university students relative to secondary school students are higher than in the U.S., Canada and Europe (table 13).

TABLE 13

AVERAGE EXPENDITURES PER PUPIL IN HIGHER EDUCATION RELATIVE TO EXPENDITURES PER PUPIL IN SECONDARY EDUCATION IN 1988 PER REGION

	Mean	Std. Dev.	Countries
For All Countries	6.07	5.63	92
Other Africa	7.06	2.96	2
Sub-Saharan Africa	10.85	6.13	22
Latin America	**4.86**	**4.17**	**15**
Caribbean and Other	6.25	7.18	11
US and Canada	1.96	.00	1
Asia	4.91	4.86	20
Europe and USSR	2.52	1.14	19
Oceania	7.67	6.41	2

Countries within the same range of per capita GNP as Latin America

	Mean	Std. Dev.	Countries
Other Africa	4.97	.00	1
Sub-Saharan Africa	8.20	5.40	8
Caribbean and Other	6.02	4.70	4
Asia	4.24	2.06	5
Europe & USSR	3.70	.86	2
Oceania	12.20	.00	1

Source: UNESCO. *World Education Report*. Santiago, Chile. 1991.

Per pupil expenditures in secondary school students are generally higher than per pupil expenditures on primary school students. Countries range from those that spend 18% of per primary pupil expenditures on secondary school students to those who spend 25 times as much on secondary students as on primary school students. Half of the countries spend at least 1.8 times as much per secondary school students as per primary school student. On average, countries spend 2.6 times as much per secondary school student as per primary school student.

On average, Latin American countries spend 50% more on every secondary school student than on every primary school student. This difference is substantially lower than in Africa, and very close to the same ratio in the Caribbean, the U.S. and Canada, Asia and Europe (table 14).

TABLE 14

AVERAGE EXPENDITURES PER PUPIL IN SECONDARY EDUCATION RELATIVE TO EXPENDITURES PER PUPIL IN PRIMARY EDUCATION IN 1988 PER REGION

	Mean	Std. Dev.	Countries
For All Countries	2.61	3.28	99
Other Africa	2.90	.56	2
Sub-Saharan Africa	5.19	5.31	28
Latin America	**1.49**	**.55**	**15**
Caribbean and Other	1.48	.83	12
US and Canada	1.50	.00	1
Asia	1.78	.79	20
Europe and USSR	1.50	.61	19
Oceania	.86	.03	2

Countries within the same range of per capita GNP as Latin America

	Mean	Std. Dev.	Countries
Other Africa	2.50	.00	1
Sub-Saharan Africa	3.48	1.50	10
Caribbean and Other	1.95	1.25	4
Asia	1.31	.51	5
Europe and USSR	1.44	.00	2
Oceania	.83	.00	1

Source: UNESCO. *World Education Report*. Santiago, Chile. 1991.

VIII. The Distribution of Education Expenditures

Education funds are used to finance different types of inputs. At one level they can be used to finance investments or recurrent expenditures, mostly teacher salaries. They can also be allocated differentially to various levels of education.

Education Expenditures by Type

Latin America spends a substantially higher proportion of education budgets for recurrent expenditures than other regions. This suggests that there are relatively fewer public resources available for school buildings and other school investments. Latin America spends a slightly smaller proportion of the recurrent budget on teacher salaries than other regions, which suggests more resources available for administration and classroom materials.

The shares allocated to primary and secondary education are lower in Latin America than in the rest of the world, while the share for higher education is higher. This, compounded by the low overall level of education spending, explains the large gap in absolute terms between Latin America and the world at the lower levels of education.

In 1988 recurrent expenditures as a percentage of education expenditures ranged from 64% to 100%. Half of the countries spent over 92% of their education budgets on recurrent expenditures; on average they spent 90% on recurrent expenditures.

Latin America is at the high end of allocations to recurrent expenditures relative to the total education budget as seen in table 15.

In the world, 50% of the countries spend 10% or more of their education budget on nonrecurrent expenditures, but in Latin America 93% of the countries spend 10% or less for this purpose. Forty-six percent of Latin American countries spend less than 5% of their education budgets on non-recurrent expenditures.

In 1988 the share of recurrent expenditures for teacher salaries ranged from 35% to 96%. Half of the countries spent 65% or more on teacher salaries. On average, countries spent 66% of their recurrent budget on teacher salaries. Latin America does not spend a higher share on teacher salaries than other regions in the world, as seen in table 16.

In 1988 the share of recurrent expenditures for primary education ranged from 18% to 94%. Half of the countries spent 44% or less on primary education. On average, countries spent 46% on primary education.

TABLE 15

**RECURRENT AS A PERCENTAGE OF EDUCATION
EXPENDITURES IN 1988**

	Mean	**Std. Dev.**	**Countries**
For All Countries	90.08%	7.40%	121
Other Africa	83.08%	8.11%	6
Sub-Saharan Africa	89.37%	10.04%	29
Latin America	**94.08%**	**4.48%**	**14**
Caribbean and Other	90.50%	7.73%	10
US and Canada	92.15%	.64%	2
Asia	87.51%	6.35%	27
Europe and USSR	91.41%	4.45%	28
Oceania	96.22%	4.37%	5

Countries within the same range of per capita GNP as Latin America

Other Africa	81.27%	7.94%	4
Sub-Saharan Africa	85.42%	10.32%	10
Caribbean and Other	86.80%	10.75%	2
Asia	85.86%	4.93%	7
Europe and USSR	88.07%	5.25%	4
Oceania	99.33%	1.15%	3

Source: UNESCO. *World Education Report.* Santiago, Chile. 1991.

Education Expenditures by Level

The share of education expenditures for primary education in Latin America is lower than the equivalent share for other regions as seen in table 17.

In 1988 the share of recurrent expenditures for secondary education ranged from 4.8% to 61%. Half of the countries spent 29% or less on secondary education. On average, countries spent 29% of their recurrent budgets on secondary education.

The share of recurrent expenditures for secondary education is also smaller in Latin America than in other regions, as seen in table 18.

In 1988 the share of recurrent expenditures for higher education ranged from .2% to 40%. Half of the countries spent 17% or less of

TABLE 16

TEACHER SALARIES AS A PERCENTAGE OF RECURRENT EXPENDITURES IN 1988

	Mean	Std. Dev.	Countries
For All Countries	66.22%	13.68%	90
Other Africa	73.30%	17.39%	2
Sub-Saharan Africa	66.82%	12.83%	25
Latin America	**64.03%**	**13.80%**	**11**
Caribbean and Other	64.47%	19.28%	8
US and Canada	51.40%	.00%	1
Asia	71.38%	10.78%	18
Europe and USSR	63.42%	14.95%	21
Oceania	63.62%	11.06%	4

Countries within the same range of per capita GNP as Latin america

	Mean	Std. Dev.	Countries
Other Africa	85.60%	.00%	1
Sub-Saharan Africa	72.19%	9.12%	10
Caribbean and Other	69.65%	28.78%	2
Asia	72.94%	10.91%	5
Europe and USSR	52.10%	11.25%	3
Oceania	58.45%	.21%	2

Source: UNESCO. *World Education Report*. Santiago, Chile. 1991.

their recurrent budgets on higher education. On average, countries spent 17% of their recurrent budgets on higher education.

The share of recurrent expenditures for higher education is higher in Latin America than in Asia, Europe, Sub-Saharan Africa and the Caribbean.

IX. The Role of Private Education

The share of students enrolled in private schools in Latin America is comparable or higher to the same figure in other regions.

In 1988 the percentage of pre-school enrollments in private centers ranged from 4% to 100%. Half of the countries had 42% or less of the enrollments at this level in private centers. On average, 49% of the children enrolled in pre-school attend private centers.

TABLE 17

PERCENTAGE OF RECURRENT EXPENDITURES
IN PRIMARY EDUCATION 1988

	Mean	Std. Dev.	Countries
For All Countries	46.15%	15.46%	118
Other Africa	50.27%	17.89%	3
Sub-Saharan Africa	46.04%	14.64%	31
Latin America	**43.14%**	**11.59%**	**16**
Caribbean and Other	49.38%	13.44%	12
US and Canada	49.65%	18.03%	2
Asia	48.52%	17.50%	24
Europe and USSR	43.83%	18.02%	27
Oceania	45.87%	14.78%	3

Countries within the same range of per capita GNP as Latin America

	Mean	Std. Dev.	Countries
Other Africa	57.60%	17.82%	2
Sub-Saharan Africa	46.47%	17.73%	12
Caribbean and Other	48.50%	14.28%	4
Asia	57.60%	18.71%	7
Europe and USSR	57.00%	11.10%	4
Oceania	44.70%	.00%	1

Source: UNESCO. *World Education Report*. Santiago, Chile. 1991.

The share of pre-school enrollment in private schools is lower in Latin America than in all other regions except the United States and Canada.

In 1988 the percentage of primary school students attending private institutions ranged from 0% to 100% in different countries. Half of the countries had less than 8% of primary school students enrolled in private schools. On average, 15% of primary school students are enrolled in private institutions.

The share of primary school children enrolled in private schools in Latin America is among the highest in the world, as seen in table 21.

In 1988 the percentage of secondary school students enrolled in private school ranged from 1% to 82%. Half the countries have 16% or

TABLE 18

SHARE OF RECURRENT EXPENDITURES FOR
SECONDARY EDUCATION IN 1988

	Mean	Std. Dev.	Countries
For All Countries	29.81%	10.64%	102
Other Africa	32.85%	6.58%	2
Sub-Saharan Africa	29.41%	10.48%	29
Latin America	**21.46%**	**9.05%**	**15**
Caribbean and Other	29.58%	7.97%	12
US and Canada	23.10%	.00%	1
Asia	31.31%	9.05%	20
Europe and USSR	35.16%	12.51%	21
Oceania	28.75%	3.04%	2

Countries within the same range of per capita GNP as Latin America

	Mean	Std. Dev.	Countries
Other Africa	37.50%	.00%	1
Sub-Saharan Africa	29.81%	8.80%	10
Caribbean and Other	27.95%	4.18%	4
Asia	25.00%	9.26%	5
Europe and USSR	19.10%	2.69%	2
Oceania	30.90%	.00%	1

Source: UNESCO. *World Education Report.* Santiago, Chile. 1991.

less of the secondary school students enrolled in private school. On average, 24% of the secondary school students attend private school.

The share of secondary school enrollments in Latin America is among the highest in the world, as seen in table 22.

X. Conclusions

On the basis of comparisons with other regions, this paper concludes that Latin America has serious problems in the financing of education, in terms of imbalances between levels, but especially in terms of overall underfinancing of the sector. It is therefore not surprising that the education systems of the region are turning out products of low quality and at great inefficiency. It is clear that as the economies of Latin America open up to compete in global markets—where comparative advantage is increasingly a function of knowledge value added—atten-

TABLE 19

**PERCENTAGE OF RECURRENT EXPENDITURES FOR
HIGHER EDUCATION IN 1988**

	Mean	Std. Dev.	Countries
For All Countries	17.06%	8.43%	111
Other Africa	20.23%	8.39%	3
Sub-Saharan Africa	17.74%	7.13%	25
Latin America	**20.26%**	**8.90%**	**16**
Caribbean and Other	7.69%	6.76%	12
US and Canada	34.30%	8.06%	2
Asia	16.97%	8.36%	24
Europe and USSR	16.05%	5.82%	26
Oceania	26.43%	7.39%	3
Countries within the same range of per capita GNP as Latin America			
Other Africa	23.30%	9.19%	2
Sub-Saharan Africa	17.63%	8.56%	10
Caribbean and Other	9.27%	8.21%	4
Asia	19.29%	8.74%	7
Europe and USSR	16.07%	3.17%	4
Oceania	17.90%	.00%	1

Source: UNESCO. *World Education Report*. Santiago, Chile. 1991.

tion to these constraints of the effectiveness and efficiency of the education systems becomes imperative.

Opportunities for Reform

While I do not propose that the solutions to the problems facing the education systems of Latin America are simply a matter of resources,[13] resources should not be underestimated either. There is a point where attempting to improve starving education systems becomes like trying to squeeze water out of stones. Furthermore, overcoming the existing "system fatigue" and turning the gradual decline of the sector back into progress will require closing the gap between the level of resources for education in Latin America and those of other regions of comparable income levels.

TABLE 20

**SHARE OF PRE-SCHOOL ENROLLMENT IN
PRIVATE SCHOOLS IN 1988**

	Mean	Std. Dev.	Countries
For All Countries	48.97%	30.96%	38
Other Africa	82.00%	23.81%	3
Sub-Saharan Africa	54.00%	32.98%	12
Latin America	**30.13%**	**17.03%**	**15**
Caribbean and Other	79.17%	18.75%	6
US and Canada	20.00%	22.63%	2
Countries within the same range of per capita GNP as Latin America			
Other Africa	95.50%	6.36%	2
Sub-Saharan Africa	52.67%	11.06%	3
Caribbean and Other	91.00%	5.66%	2

Source: UNESCO. *World Education Report.* Santiago, Chile. 1991.

A comparative perspective—though limited to the extent that data are not available for all countries of the world—is useful to place the patterns observed in the region in context. For instance, a recent World Bank report on education and human resources for Latin America states:

> The key issue within the sector is the inefficient resource allocation between public spending on primary education on the one hand and tertiary education on the other. In most LAC countries, government subsidies still tend to favor tertiary education despite the fact that primary and pre-school education given higher returns per dollar or peso spent. For LAC as a whole, in 1989, higher education costs were subsidized at a rate seven times greater than those for primary education.[14]

However, the report fails to indicate that for countries with income levels falling within the range of income levels of Latin America, the same ratio of subsidies for tertiary to primary students is 26 in Sub-Saharan Africa, 14 in the Caribbean and 6 in Asia. The same report also fails to indicate that there has been a steady trend in Latin America to reduce those imbalances during the last 30 years. For instance, while the

TABLE 21

SHARE OF PRIMARY SCHOOL ENROLLMENT IN
PRIVATE SCHOOLS IN 1988

	Mean	Std. Dev.	Countries
For All Countries	15.34%	21.40%	59
Other Africa	9.33%	12.74%	3
Sub-Saharan Africa	16.86%	26.65%	29
Latin America	**16.81%**	**15.92%**	**16**
Caribbean and Other	11.56%	16.07%	9
US and Canada	7.50%	4.95%	2
Countries within the same range of per capita GNP as Latin America			
Other Africa	2.00%	1.41%	2
Sub-Saharan Africa	38.44%	39.74%	9
Caribbean and Other	3.00%	1.83%	4

Source: UNESCO. *World Education Report.* Santiago, Chile. 1991.

ratio of tertiary per pupil expenditure to primary per pupil expenditure was 16.6 in 1965, it declined to 13.6 in 1970, 11.5 in 1975 and to 7.8 in 1978.[15] Also ignored in the report is the fact that Latin America has achieved greater *access* to each level of education than most countries with comparable income levels. While there are problems that need to be addressed, this should be done without jeopardizing this comparative advantage.

The evidence examined supports the conclusion that Latin America invests less per student at all levels than most regions of the world and that this gap between Latin America and the rest of the world is growing.

The paradox of lower spending levels in absolute terms and relative to income levels in the region, while the level of effort of the governments is comparable to that of other regions, leads to the conclusion that one of the problems undermining the education sector is the low tax base with which governments operate.

A critical issue then is to achieve a significant increase in education resources at all levels. This will not be achieved by transfers of existing resources between levels, for it would further increase the gap in per

TABLE 22

SHARE OF SECONDARY SCHOOL ENROLLMENT IN
PRIVATE SCHOOLS IN 1988

	Mean	Std. Dev.	Countries
For All Countries	24.33%	20.98%	52
Other Africa	10.00%	5.29%	3
Sub-Saharan Africa	26.08%	22.72%	25
Latin America	**31.57%**	**20.45%**	**14**
Caribbean and Other	15.87%	16.77%	8
US and Canada	7.00%	1.41%	2

Countries within the same range of per capita GNP as Latin America

	Mean	Std. Dev.	Countries
Other Africa	8.00%	5.66%	2
Sub-Saharan Africa	43.00%	26.04%	7
Caribbean and Other	4.67%	3.05%	3

Source: UNESCO. *World Education Report*. Santiago, Chile. 1991.

pupil expenditure between Latin America and the rest of the world.[16] Rather *additional* resources must be generated for education at all levels.

Options to increase resources for education include increasing the share of education in the government budget. This would mean increasing the level of effort of government for the sector beyond that of other sectors. The critical question here is what should be sacrificed for education's sake. To the extent that education gains resources currently spent in less productive activities, such as defense or internal security, for instance, the costs of this adjustment will be lesser than if resources were transferred from other important sectors such as agriculture, health, housing or transportation.

Another option is to maintain the level of education relative to total government expenditures, increasing the tax base and the overall levels of spending of the government. This option would be inconsistent with the current trend of "less government."

A mixed option would be increasing government resources, but only for education, which would require broadening the tax base and targeting the additional resources for education. This trend is consistent with proposals to reduce the scope of activities where the government intervenes, but to concentrate government action in areas with externalities and where the government has a comparative advantage, such as education, health, construction of roads, etc.[17]

Other options for expanding resources include promoting private contributions, either in the form of additional financing from beneficiaries of education (tuition fees), or promoting the expansion of private schools. As will be discussed later, neither of these options is an appropriate response to generate additional resources at the basic levels in the current context of Latin America.

An option to generate additional resources for a particular level or type of education is to transfer resources from other levels. Given the underfinancing of expenditures at all levels, this option is not considered an appropriate response to the problems facing the education *system*, nor is it considered more feasible than transferring funds, for example, out of the Ministry of Defense and into the Ministry of Education.

The distribution of public education expenditures by type is not particularly different from those of other regions. However, Latin America spends a higher percentage of public education funds for tertiary education than other regions, to the detriment of other levels of education. While this reflects the greater effort made in Latin America to expand educational opportunity at the tertiary level, it also suggests inequitable use of public funds, since students at this level have a higher capacity to contribute to the cost of their education than students at lower levels of education.

The shares going to different levels of education should be changed in favor of basic and secondary education, but this should be done in the context of a growing education budget, and not draining resources from universities. A recent study of the World Bank is consistent with this assessment stating that per pupil expenditure in higher education in Latin America is not excessive:

> Higher education in Latin America has gone through difficult fiscal times. Real expenditures per pupil have decreased, non-personnel outlays have diminished, and, by inference, undergraduate instructional quality has declined. Strong arguments can be given that per pupil expenditures should be increased, but existing misallocation of resources provides no assurance that additional spending would be used efficiently.[18]

The existing evidence offers no reason to expect significant gains in resources from further privatization of education, a frequently touted option for the sector. Latin America is at the high end of enrollments in private institutions at all levels. The development of private schools could be promoted by reducing the negative incentives that currently stem from excessive government regulation (e.g., caps on tuition fees, excessive paper work and "permisology," which gives supervisors of the private school system the ability to harass private schools, particularly small government non-elite schools that lack the political clout to protect themselves).

Promoting privatization, however, is a good option which favors more efficient utilization of existing resources rather than generating additional resources. Channelling public funds to privately managed schools serving poor children (such as the *Fe y Alegría* program) or establishing matching funds to support schools serving poor children are options to promote privatization.

The option of generating additional resources at the basic levels by charging tuition fees in public schools should be carefully considered. Most public schools already have some forms of "voluntary" contributions from parents. Further cost-recovery at primary and secondary education levels should not be introduced unless appropriate studies of price elasticity of demand are made to anticipate the impact on equity and the expected gains in levels of resources. It may be desirable to increase cost-recovery at the tertiary level, with mechanisms that ensure that this does not discourage enrollments from needy students, but this is more justifiable as a strategy to increase the internal efficiency of the sub-sector by placing incentives to encourage early completion rather than as a substitute for public expenditures on the sector.

The impact of financial constraints is compounded by the fast pace with which Ministries of Education have had to adjust to rapid changes during the last decade. The economic crisis that affected most countries of the region during the 1980s had an important toll on the education sector.

This toll, and the "system fatigue" it generated in Ministries of Education, is a constraint to options to improve the use of existing resources. In the short run additional resources will be necessary to fuel reforms designed to make better use of resources. But at the same time, additional resources should not be "thrown" at fatigued systems. Fresh resources should be used as opportunities to promote improvements in quality and internal efficiency, not to promote more of the same. For instance, it is quite possible that in systems with large rates of repetition, quality improvements in the forms of textbooks, instructional supplies and better teacher training over time will pay for themselves.[19] However, developing these new instructional materials and providing them in the short run means additional up front investment before any savings from reduced repetition have been realized.

One of the priorities to achieve more resources for education and better utilization of existing resources is to develop the capacity in Ministries of Education for policy analysis, program preparation and budgeting and financial control. Many Ministries of Education lack the ability to establish priorities for action and to develop appropriate programs and budgets that can persuade Ministries of Finance to fund them. In addition, Ministries of Education have institutional constraints to disburse funds allocated to them or to respond effectively to the spending disincentives implemented by Ministries of Finance. As a result, it is hard for the sector to justify increases in allocations for nonsalary activities when assigned budgets are not spent.

Some of the options to improve internal efficiency include exploring alternative configurations of education inputs (e.g., more textbooks and less-trained teachers, teachers with less specialized training, more parental participation). Changing the mix of inputs may also reduce costs, but this should be done with the explicit goal of increasing efficiency rather than just cutting costs (e.g., developing new teaching technologies relying more on peer teaching and instructional materials, which allow increasing class size, or developing new teaching career structures to give more incentives to skill improvement rather than to credentials, seniority or political connections, promoting new forms of local management, transferring some of the tasks now handled by large and inefficient central bureaucracies to more decentralized levels).

Other options include increasing the efficiency in the use of existing inputs, such as giving priority to the assignment of new teachers to understaffed schools, or establishing systems to encourage the better trained teachers to attend the early grades where school failure is higher, or channeling instructional resources to the early grades of primary school to reduce repetition rates.

Significant gains in the efficiency of higher education could be achieved by changing the formulae used for the allocation of public funds between universities. Typically, existing allocation practices reflect political weight and institutional tradition rather than the quality of graduates or the number of years it takes different institutions to produce a graduate. New criteria could provide incentives to encourage research, quality education, closer ties between programs and demands of the market, and on-time completion. University governance is another area that could benefit from innovations to move away from the deep-rooted systems of patron-client relationships and from the control of universities by strong political and interest groups toward more accountability and professional management.

Gains in efficiency and quality at the basic levels could be attained by developing combined schemes of publicly funded, but privately managed educational alternatives. An example is the *Fe y Alegría* schools which operate in 12 countries of the region and reputedly do a much better job than the State at providing quality education to the poor.[20]

Strengthening the ties between schools and communities is an attractive option, not to generate additional resources—which may not be feasible given the scenario described later—but to improve the utilization of existing resources, to establish accountability from teachers to the community and to monitor teacher attendance and performance.[21]

The Changing Context of the 1980s

The 1980s were a decade of growing austerity in Latin America which reduced the potential contributions of households to education. Adjusting countries also reduced public education expenditures. Facing reductions in funds, education ministries disproportionately cut the share for teaching materials. Eventually, teacher salaries deteriorated in real terms too.

The announcement in 1982 that Mexico could not continue servicing its foreign debt obligations marked a rupture with the environment-facing governments in the Third World. As it became clear that many countries had been borrowing (and banks lending) too much, commercial banks became more reluctant to lend money. Faced with mounting pressure from interest payments, countries turned to multilateral banks who were willing to lend them more funds to support efforts to stabilize and adjust their economies. For many nations, economic adjustment was the hallmark of the 1980s.

Adjustment programs have had a relatively short-term focus, mostly because adjustment was initially thought to be a short-term problem. A UNICEF study for Latin America points out:

> The experience with adjustment programmes, however, has not been satisfactory. While these programmes should not be seen as the cause of the economic decline of the 1980s, they clearly have not been able to reverse the adverse developments in the living standards of the poor, nor in most cases have they led to resumed economic growth. In addition, these adjustment programmes have generally made no explicit efforts to prevent deteriorations in human conditions. Thus there is still considerable debate on the possibility of contin-

uing progress in health, nutrition and education under these adverse economic conditions and on the nature of the macro-economic policies and health measures needed to foster such progress.[22]

There are two basic channels through which adjustment can influence education.

The first is through the impact of adjustment on households. As policies succeed at contracting aggregate demand, the living conditions of many people deteriorate, thereby reducing the income they have available for school supplies (uniforms, tuition, textbooks, etc.) and increasing the need for children to contribute to the household economy.

This type of impact would influence external and internal efficiency and equity. Poorer families would have to pull their children out of school. The reduction in the ability of households to contribute could also lead to internal inefficiencies not only from the reductions in inputs available to learning, but also because of diminished efficiency in the mix of inputs. For instance the effectiveness of teacher instructional practices may be reduced if students have no textbooks or notebooks.

A second mechanism linking economic adjustment and education provision is the change in public education finance that results from pressures to reduce public spending. Overall cuts in public spending may lead to disproportionate cuts in education expenditures vis-a-vis other government expenditures.

The short-term structural rigidities in the education budget make it easier to cut certain items such as funds for teaching materials or school repairs. This has a negative impact on the internal efficiency of education as it leads to inefficient changes in the mix of inputs. It is difficult for teachers to compensate for deteriorating buildings, or to preserve educational quality when there is a lack of textbooks and materials.

There are also institutional rigidities that can lead to reductions in total resources for education, increasing inequities in educational spending. For instance, urban students and schools are typically more vocal, better organized and closer to the distribution centers of the Ministry of Education. Hence, reductions in the available instructional supplies are likely to be faced with increased pressures from those parents to preserve their initial allotments, thus increasing their share of a declining total pie. The implication is that rural schools, or those attended by students whose parents have less political leverage, will have to face disproportionate reductions in their supply of chalk and other learning resources.[23] Similarly, universities have more leverage (political and technical) to increase their share in a shrinking pie of total resources for education.

The 1980s were a decade of growing austerity in Latin America as per capita income declined in 78% of the countries. As a result, living conditions deteriorated in many countries. This is important as it effectively reduced the capacity of households to support the work of the school. The implication is that in a scenario of austerity-facing households the efforts of the State to maintain the same levels of education provision should be more, not less.

In highly unequitable economies, declining income per capita may lead to further inequities. For Latin America, some authors have proposed that a series of negative multipliers would translate a 5 to 10% reduction in GNP into a reduction three to four times larger for low income families. This notion stems from "the fact that minimum wages drop faster than do average wages, that the prices of essentials are subject to greater increases than is the Consumer Price Index, that the newly unemployed frequently also suffer the loss of health coverage and that cuts in public expenditures are typically asymmetrical. In terms of child welfare, these biases are further aggravated by the fact that poorer families generally have a larger than average number of children."[24]

In Latin America real salaries in manufacturing declined 8.4% between 1980 and 1985. Salaries in construction declined 19%, the minimum salary declined 11% and informal sector earnings declined 27% (Ibid, 19). Between 1981 and 1988 urban minimum wages in real terms declined 33% in Brazil, 46% in Mexico, and 40% in Peru.

All of these changes increase the marginal contribution of the work of children to poor households (even if their work will generate less income because of reduced demand) and diminish the ability of parents to further contribute to education by paying for school supplies, uniforms and making in-kind or cash contributions to the school. The combined effect of these factors is to increase the pressure to pull children out of school and send them to work.

Facing reductions in funds, education ministries disproportionately cut the share for teaching materials. Eventually teacher salaries deteriorated in real terms too. This made the provision of education more difficult, not just because teachers saw class sizes increase, but because it changed the organization of the teaching process: teachers had less time to prepare classes, fewer resources for teaching, taught in buildings in increasing disrepair, and faced students tired from increasing household responsibilities, sometimes hungry and sick and with fewer things to bring from home, such as notebooks and textbooks, that could help them learn. To what extent was education still possible under these circumstances? This question is not rhetorical, for it is possible that declines of education quality beyond a minimum threshold would lead parents to reassess the relative benefits of sending their children to school.

It is in this context that the low levels of education finance in Latin America and the exploration of policy options should be considered, for this context gives the growing gap between levels of education finance in Latin America and the world crisis proportions. It will take leadership to recognize the danger in this crisis and to construct opportunities for change.

APPENDIX 1

REGIONAL GROUPINGS USED IN THE STUDY

Other Africa

Algeria, Egypt, Libya, Morocco, Namibia, South Africa, Togo, Tunisia

Sub-Saharan Africa

Angola, Benin, Botswana, Burkina Faso, Burundi, Cameroon, Cape Verde, Central African Republic, Chad, Comoros, Congo, Cote D'Ivoire, Djibouti, Equatorial Guinea, Ethiopia, Gabon, Gambia, Ghana, Guinea, Guinea-Bissau, Kenya, Lesotho, Liberia,

Madagascar, Malawi, Mali, Mauritania, Mauritius, Mozambique, Niger, Nigeria, Rwanda, Sao Tome and Principe, Senegal, Seychelles, Sierra Leone, Somalia, Sudan, Swaziland, Tanzania, Uganda, Zaire, Zambia, Zimbabwe

Latin America

Argentina, Bolivia, Brazil, Chile, Colombia, Costa Rica, Cuba, Dominican Republic, Ecuador, El Salvador, Guatemala, Haiti, Honduras, Mexico, Nicaragua, Panama, Paraguay, Peru, Uruguay, Venezuela

Caribbean and Other Central and South America

Antigua, Bahamas, Barbados, Belize, British Virgin Islands, Dominica, Grenada, Guyana, Jamaica, Netherlands, St. Kitts, St. Lucia, St. Vincent, Suriname, Trinidad

United States and Canada

Canada, United States

Asia

Afghanistan, Bahrain, Bangladesh, Bhutan, Cambodia, China, Cyprus, Hong Kong, India, Indonesia, Iraq, Iran, Israel, Japan, Jordan, Korea Democratic, Korea Republic, Kuwait, Laos, Lebanon, Malaysia, Maldives, Mongolia, Myanmar, Nepal, Oman, Pakistan,

Palestine, Philippines, Qatar, Saudi Arabia, Singapore, Sri Lanka, Syria, Thailand, Turkey, United Arab Emirates, Vietnam, Yemen

Europe and Former Soviet Republics

Albania, Austria, Belgium, Bulgaria, Czechoslovakia, Denmark, Finland, France, Germany Democratic Republic, Germany Federal Republic, Greece, Hungary, Iceland, Ireland, Italy, Luxembourg, Malta, Monaco, Netherlands, Norway, Poland, Portugal, Romania, San Marino, Spain, Sweden, Switzerland, USSR, United Kingdom, Yugoslavia,

Oceania

Australia, Fiji Kribati, New Zealand, Oceania, Papua New Guinea, Samoa, Tonga

NOTES

1. The country with the lowest per capita income in Latin America in 1989 had US$ 400 per capita, and the highest US$ 2,620. Most tables include separate comparative information for countries in each region which fall within this range of per capita income. This excludes the poorest 25% and the richest 30% countries in the world.

2. World Bank, *World Development Report 1990* (New York: Oxford University Press, 1990).

3. W. Elley, *How in the World Do Students Read?* (International Association for the Evaluation of Educational Achievement, 1992).

4. A. Lapointe et al., *Learning Science*, Report No. 22 (IAEP, 1992).

5. F. Reimers et al., *Análisis del sistema educativo en el Paraguay. Sugerencias de política y estrategia para su reforma* (Asunción: HIID-CPES, 1992).

6. E. Schiefelbein, "Financing Education for Democracy in Latin America" (Santiago, Chile: 1991). Mimeo.

7. G. Guevara, "México: Un país de reprobados", *Nexos* (June 1992): 33-44.

8. E. Schiefelbein, *Repetition Rates: The Key Issue in South American Primary Education* (Washington, DC: The World Bank, LATHR Division, 1988).

9. The World Bank, *Costa Rica. Public Sector Social Spending* (Washington, DC: The World Bank, 1990) 19.

10. Derived from table 22, page 53. UNESCO-OREALC, *Situación educativa de América Latina y el Caribe. 1980-1987* (Santiago, Chile: UNESCO, 1990).

11. These figures are for 1985. T. Tovar, *Ser maestro. Condiciones del trabajo docente en Perú* (Lima, Peru: UNESCO-DESCO, 1989).

12. F. Reimers, *Education Policy Priorities in Guatemala. An Agenda for Policy Dialogue* (Guatemala City: 1993) 24.

13. For a discussion of a systemic agenda for education reform, involving the areas of finance, management and products of education, see F. Reimers, *A New Scenario for Educational Planning and Management in Latin America* (Paris: UNESCOInternational Institute for Educational Planning, 1990).

14. The World Bank, *Human Resources in Latin America and the Caribbean* (Washington, DC: The World Bank, 1993) 52-53.

15. E. Schiefelbein, *Education Costs and Financing Policies in Latin America* (Washington, DC: World Bank, 1987) 7.

16. It should be noted that countries of comparable income levels in Asia spend 20% more per primary school student, and in the Caribbean five times more per primary student than countries in Latin America. A similar gap exists for secondary students (where Asia spends 20% more, the Caribbean 2.4 times more and Sub-Saharan Africa 1.8 times more than Latin America) and for university students (where Asia spends 52% more per student, the Caribbean 3.4 times more per student, and Sub-Saharan Africa 3.64 times more than Latin America).

17. The World Bank, *World Development Report 1991* (Washington, DC: Oxford University Press, 1991).

18. D. Winkler, *Higher Education in Latin America. Issues of Efficiency and Equity* (Washington, DC: World Bank Discussion Papers, 1990) 30.

19. This is, for instance, what was found in the Northeast of Brazil, see R. Harbison and E. Hanushek, *Educational Performance of the Poor: Lessons from Rural Northeast Brazil* (Oxford: Oxford University Press, 1992).

20. A study of this program in Guatemala found that 85% of the students who enter pre-school in *Fe y Alegría* complete six grades in seven years, in contrast with 34% completion rates in the same period in Government schools. See J. Diaz, *La educación subvencionada. Un modelo de opción para la educación nacional* (Guatemala: Universidad del Valle de Guatemala, Facultad de Educación, 1989) 67.

21. There are three educational innovations in Latin America that provide quality education to the poor where strengthened school-community relations play a critical role, see F. Reimers, *Education and the Consolidation of Democracy in Latin America. Innovations to Provide Quality Education with Equity* (Washington, DC: Academy for Educational Development, Project EHRTS, 1993).

22. T. Albanez, E. Bustelo, G. Cornia and E. Jepersen, *Economic Decline and Child Survival: The Plight of Latin America in the Eighties* (Florence: UNICEF, Innocenti Occasional Papers, 1989) 1.

23. For a study of how Ministries of Education responded to budget cuts see F. Reimers, "Tiene Jomtien relevancia en América Latina. Los ajustes a la educación cuando se ajusta la economía", *La Educación* 35.108-110 (1991): 101-132.

24. T. Albanez, E. Bustelo, G. Cornia and E. Jepersen, *Economic Decline and Child Survival: The Plight of Latin America in the Eighties* (Florence: UNICEF, Innocenti Occasional Papers, 1989) 17-18.

EDUCATIONAL COOPERATION
IN THE AMERICAS:
A REVIEW

Joseph P. Farrell[*]

SUMMARY

This paper provides a critical analysis of the role played by international cooperation, particularly multilateral and bilateral donor agencies, in support of large-scale educational reform programs in Latin America and the Caribbean. It is argued that most major educational reform programs have failed or had limited success. A review of what has been learned about designing and implementing educational reform provides a framework for examining the record regarding the contribution of international cooperation. It is argued that contribution has for the most part been negative. A list is provided of common counterproductive behaviors among donor agencies. An alternate model of international cooperation, labeled "horizontal intellectual cooperation," is described. It is finally argued that while large-scale national reform is difficult, school-level change is relatively easy. A useful role for international cooperation would be to assist in learning from many small-scale successful changes and to stimulate *local capacity to innovate*.

Introduction

The letter from Jeff Puryear and José Joaquín Brunner that sets out the specifications for this review paper states the following: "Specifically, we would like you to prepare a comprehensive background memorandum that reviews experience with educational cooperation and

---

[*] Dr. Farrell is currently Head of the Comparative, International and Development Education Centre, and Professor in the Department of Adult Education at the Ontario Institute for Studies in Education. He received his Ph.D. in Comparative Education from Syracuse University. He has authored and co-authored several books and articles in the field of educational development including *Teacher Development in Developing Nations*, *Textbooks in Developing Countries: Economic and Education Choices*, and *The National Unified Schools in Allende's Chile: The Role of Education in the Destruction of a Revolution*.

assistance between North and South America, with the goal of identifying current deficiencies and suggesting new modalities. Your memorandum should look carefully at existing forms of educational cooperation and aid at the bilateral and regional level, take note of strengths and weaknesses, and suggest improvements." In addition, I am referred to the Dialogue's report, *Convergence and Community; The Americas in 1993*, the proposal for this educational task force, and, as a "benchmark for our initiative," the UNESCO-CEPAL document, *Education and Knowledge: Basic Pillars of Changing Production Patterns with Social Equity*. Reference to these documents is useful since they provide the context—the view of the future—through which any observations and recommendations I might make will be seen. However, in reviewing the "predictions" about the future contained explicitly or implicitly in these background documents, and comparing them to my own sense of where things are going, I am reminded of an old (possibly apocryphal) Chinese proverb: "Prediction is always difficult; especially with respect to the future." There are some of those predictions with which I agree (which means mainly that I share at least some of the biases of those who have made them), and some with which I disagree (which means that I don't share all of those biases). The matter is important to note at the outset because some of the differences lead to differing conclusions about appropriate educational policy and, consequently, to different notions about directions and modalities for educational cooperation.

I will at this introductory point provide only a few key examples of such differences of view of the future with attendant educational implications. On p. 1 of the master proposal it is claimed that one of the problems with Latin American educational systems is that they have "proved unresponsive to rapidly changing labor markets." Further down the same page the document states: "Open economies integrated into the global system require an internationally competitive labor force with an emphasis on science and technology." In all three documents the educational implications drawn from those claims are then drawn out primarily, if not exclusively, with reference to the *formal school systems* of the region.

There are several problems with this chain of analysis. First, if labor markets are indeed "rapidly changing," as they appear to be, then formal school systems which take from one to two decades to convert a first grade student into a labor market entrant, will by definition be unresponsive to such rapid changes. Less formal occupational training systems, operated by enterprises and nonformal education agencies, are required. Second, those labor market changes which are occurring do not provide a strong case for a "science and technology" emphasis for most students.

Evidence from the United States, based on projections by the American Bureau of Labor Statistics, indicates that while the greatest *proportional* growth will be in occupations demanding high levels of education and specialized training, particularly in science and technology, the greatest *number* of new jobs will be created in occupational categories which require minimal formal education. And the evidence regarding the "deskilling" of many such job categories suggests that many of those new jobs will require even less formal education in the future than they do now (Bailey 1991). Canadian occupational projections show much the same story. Well over half of all new jobs estimated to be created by the mid-1990s will be low level, increasingly deskilled, educationally undemanding positions. The five largest categories of new jobs are predicted to be (in order) sales clerks, bank cashiers and tellers, secretaries, clerks, and truck drivers (COPS 1990). Can one realistically expect the pattern to be different in Latin America? Indeed, the major concern among many North American workers is that the low tech, increasingly deskilled heavy manufacturing jobs will be those which are "exported south." Moreover, what is one really talking about when referring to a "modern workplace" for most Latin American workers? Can one really imagine that the millions of Latin American peasants, or their children, will find themselves in the foreseeable future in a "modern workplace" which is heavily science/technology dependent? Or the children of the millions of urban slum dwellers? Or the parentless street kids? Surely there is a need for more—and more sophisticated—science and technology knowledge among that relatively small minority of young people in *both* North and South America who are likely to end up in high-level managerial and research/development/entrepreneurial positions. And clearly it would be desirable for all people in *all* of the Americas to have a better basic understanding of "science." But while these are worthy goals, little is known about how to provide such general science understanding to the population not pursuing careers in scientific fields, and we in North America have very little to teach the rest of the hemisphere about how to do this. There have been many experiments but little solid evidence of widespread impact. What both of the observations above indicate is that responses to the changing nature of the world economy, and the position of all of the American nations in it, are likely to require much more emphasis on out-of-school-based knowledge creation and transmittal systems. Generally speaking, these are more likely to be designed and run effectively by nongovernmental than by governmental delivery systems. If this is the case, then forms of international cooperation which assume or depend upon government-to-government or international agency-to-government relationships are likely to be quite *ineffective*, and quite new forms of cooperation arrangements will have to be invented.

There is a further general problem with these background documents. There is an air of certainty about them, with respect to the future, and with respect to the current and desired future state of education over the entire hemisphere, which is somewhere between chutzpa and hubris. Surely if any of us once thought that we could make reasonably certain claims about how the future would unfold, particularly at the level of national and international economics and politics, the experience of the past few years should have disabused us of that notion. The confident claims about the future in these documents strike this reader as more nearly a neo-liberal wish list than anything else. Certainly there has been movement toward a more openly competitive and integrated international economy over the past few years, but the forces of national (or regional) protectionism are still strong, and which way things will actually go is still an open question. As of this writing (November 1993) it is not clear whether the North American Free Trade Agreement (NAFTA) will actually be approved by all three of the nations involved. The U.S. has just approved it, but with many concessions to strong protectionist forces, and Canada has still not agreed. The eventual fate of the Uruguay Round of the GATT remains uncertain. The farm subsidy war between the United States and the European community, which is savaging the agricultural industry in Canada and much of the developing world, rages on. For every economist who confidently claims that we are beginning to emerge from the near-worldwide recession one can find another who will equally confidently claim that recovery will be a very long time coming, or indeed that things will get much worse before they begin to get better. Now, I have my own personal preferences on these matters, but I learned a long time ago not to assume that the world will necessarily work out as I would like it to. And I would not want to recommend that any nation of the Americas stake its educational policy on the assumption that one particular vision of the economic future will come to pass. Rather, one should be thinking of policies, and forms of cooperation, which will be useful across a wide range of possible futures. It turns out that many of the policy suggestions found in these documents do fit that prescription, but not all do.

There is a broader and deeper trend related to the above which may have a very profound impact on the ways we even think about educational policy and international cooperation. These background documents stress the "techno-economic" impacts of recent and ongoing technological change. What is not noted clearly is the *political* impact, the effect upon the very definition of the nation-state. Educational policy is a means by which states control and regulate the provision of opportunities to learn in organized ways among (at least) the young, and increasingly among adults. That is, it is an instrument of *statecraft*. There are several different models or theories of "the state," but all assume the modern concept of the nation-state which arose in Europe two to three centuries ago and which has become well-nigh universal.

Educational policy is a *national* activity, except in some federal states such as Canada where it is partly or wholly the responsibility of lower levels of government which for purposes of education behave like nation-states. But in the early 1990s many of the assumed basic characteristics of the nation-state appear to be changing. In an era where technology permits the essentially instantaneous transfer of huge amounts of capital from almost anywhere and any currency to anywhere, no nation has sovereign and autonomous control over its fiscal and monetary policy—as Sweden and the United Kingdom learned very recently. Cultural systems and symbols are rapidly becoming as easily transferred internationally as is capital. The technical wizards claim that we are a very short time away from the point where almost anyone anywhere in the world with the price of a cheap VCR can buy a small dish antenna which will give them access directly in their home to television signals from almost everywhere in the world, with no form of state regulation or control effectively possible. What does national cultural sovereignty mean in such circumstances? Those who have thought about such patterns at all in the past have tended to think in terms of some form of "dependency" theory. It appears that we are moving rapidly toward a situation where *all* nations are to a rather high degree *dependent* nations; where all states have less and less effective control over their economies, their societies or their polities. When these patterns are combined with a widespread growth of sub-national loyalties they are in many cases leading to the literal disintegration (in the precise meaning of that word: dis-integration) of nation states.

In a recent book Fuller (1991) uses the term "fragile state" to refer to conditions in many developing nations. It appears that currently *all* nations, rich or poor, are becoming increasingly fragile states. A further complication in many parts of Latin America, and in Canada, is that among many sub-national groups (indigenous peoples, for example, or a significant portion of Quebec society) there has never been a full acceptance of the power or legitimacy of the nation-state in which they live. Migdal, in his aptly titled book *Strong Societies and Weak States* (1987), observes that in such cases one frequently has a condition in which the various societies within a polity are stronger than the fragile nation-state which putatively encompasses them. All of this most profoundly challenges previous understandings of what educational policy *is*, and what it is *about*, but the implications are not yet at all clear. What does it really mean to plan education as an instrument of *national* economic, social, or cultural policy in such circumstances? What does it mean to talk of inter*national* cooperation when the various national entities involved are becoming increasingly fragile?

One possible implication for the main theme of this paper is the following. International agencies (e.g., the development banks and national aid agencies such as CIDA and USAID) work ordinarily or exclusively at the level of the fragile state. It is usually nongovernmental organizations which work with what Migdal calls the "strong societies" within the fragile states. This may have, and may increasingly have, the perverse effect of channelling the largest flows of international cooperation resources at the level where they can have the least effect, or may indeed have counterproductive effects. I will cite here just one example of how this perverse effect can work, which I know from personal experience. In a Latin American nation (which I will not name) a textbook development and distribution program partially funded by an international agency ran into difficulties in delivering the books in many rural villages because an ongoing "insurgency" (read civil war pitting indigenous peoples and very poor mestizo villagers against the "national" government) had effectively destroyed most of the transportation infrastructure and made life quite dangerous for any "agents" of the national government, however well-intentioned. I was told proudly by government officials and officials of the international agency that the problem had been solved by using the national armed forces, whose jeeps, trucks, and helicopters could reach even the most remote portions of the national territory, to deliver the textbooks. It never occurred to them that what this meant was that the textbooks, which "naturally" carried "national" messages and symbols, were being delivered by those who were, in the villagers' experience, the "nation's" main agents among them of death and destruction. I was told later by several literacy/community development workers with an NGO active in the villages that the symbolism had not been lost on the local people. The textbooks were rejected in the villages and their arrival led even more families to withdraw their children from the village schools. This is of course an extreme example, but as with extreme examples generally it serves to starkly outline the difficulties possible when working internationally with fragile states rather than strong societies.

One possible response to this general condition (or at least what might be seen as such a response) is the move toward "decentralization," often encouraged and supported through international cooperation. This approach is cited and lauded in the master proposal for this dialogue. I personally support it (but not in all cases; it is an often useful tool but not a universal nostrum). However, decentralization as usually conceived misconstrues the problem. Decentralization normally refers to the devolution by the central state authority of various forms of power and control to lower, more localized levels of government. But if the central state is itself weak and becoming weaker, then there is less and less *effective* power and control to devolve, such that the entire exercise becomes increasingly empty and meaningless (rather like a person with little or no wealth going to great lengths to write a will governing what the heirs will inherit).

In sum, I am arguing that the most profound, and yet very poorly understood, effects of the international changes we are parties and witnesses to are not in the technical or economic realms, but in the most basic constructs we normally use to frame discussions of educational policy and international educational cooperation in the Americas. In the spirit of humility about predicting the future noted above, I make no claim to have a clear idea of what this all means or where it will lead us. But I do assert that any "dialogue" about educational policy and international cooperation in support of it which does not from the outset systematically attend to these changes is almost certain to be irrelevant to the conditions in which school children and adult learners in the 1990s will actually live out their lives.

One thing which these background documents emphasize however, and this is a point with which I entirely agree, is that when thinking about how to "strengthen international cooperation to improve educational systems throughout the region" (Puryear's letter of 5 February 1993 to me), we are not for the most part thinking about modest changes in such educational systems. The question to be addressed is what has been learned about how international cooperation may strengthen (or, conversely, weaken) national efforts at *major and fundamental reform* of educational systems in the Americas. To deal with this question one must first examine *what has been learned about how to design and implement large-scale and fundamental educational reforms.* Put simply, if we wish international cooperation to serve educational reform, we first have to understand educational reform itself. The section which follows reviews the experience regarding educational reform attempts in both rich and poor nations, noting *inter alia* some patterns or characteristics of international cooperation which have been either supportive or destructive of such reform efforts.

Designing and Implementing Educational Reform

We now have more than thirty years of experience with attempts to design and implement large-scale, long-term programs of educational reform in Latin America and other "developing" nations, often with the assistance of multi-lateral or bi-lateral donor agencies, and considerable experience with educational reform attempts in rich nations as well. During the past few years several major works have appeared attempting to summarize various aspects of the knowledge acquired from that experience. (for example, Bryson 1988; Caillods 1989; Fagerlind and Sjosted 1990; Ginsburg 1991; Klees 1989; Rondinelli, et al. 1990; Ross and Mahlick 1990; Farrell 1989b; Farrell, in press). However, much of the available knowledge is still in the form of "lore," the experience-based wisdom of those who have been attempting to produce educational change. The observations below are based both on such published distillations and on such "lore," as I am aware.

One general lesson is that educational reform is a far more difficult and risk-prone venture than had been imagined thirty years ago. There are far more examples of failure, or of minimal success, than of relatively complete success. We know far more about what doesn't work, or doesn't usually work, than we do about what does work. A central lesson learned is that Nicolo Machiavelli was correct when he wrote more than four centuries ago: "And it ought to be remembered that there is nothing more difficult to take in hand, more perilous to conduct, or more uncertain in its success, than to take the lead in the introduction of a new order of things." The innovator has on one hand staunch enemies among "all those who have done well under the old conditions" and who see clearly an immediate threat to their privilege, but only "lukewarm defenders" among the intended beneficiaries of the change, since the putative benefits are uncertain in a dimly perceived future; and people generally "do not readily believe in new things until they have had a long experience of them" (Machiavelli 1952 [1513], 9). Moreover, when educational reform attempts have been successful, the process has usually taken a long time, frequently far longer than originally anticipated. There are in the experience of the past decades a few examples where an unusual combination of favorable conditions and politically skilled innovators have permitted a great deal of educational change to occur in a relatively brief period, but these are relatively rare and idiosyncratic. A motto which could well be hung on the walls above the desks of those attempting educational reform is: "T T T: Things Take Time." These introductory comments are not meant as a counsel of despair, but as a note of salutary caution. One can learn a great deal from failure, and combining that with knowledge gained from less common successes permits a number of observations about reform strategies and approaches, and modes of international cooperation to assist them, which are likely to be more effective and successful than others. But there are few certainties and no guarantees.

Another general lesson is that there is no single blueprint or strategy for designing and implementing educational reform which will "work" in all circumstances. There are some general principles or guidelines which are often applicable, but detailed design and planning must be based upon wisdom derived from a *solid knowledge of local conditions*. This observation is particularly salient for a paper such as this which is to relate to the very different nations and societies which constitute the "Americas." International cooperation has often been helpful in identifying and bringing to the foreground such locally based knowledge, and in building systems of institutions which can serve as on-going sources of creation and dissemination of such locally based knowledge. One thinks, for example, of the very useful support provided by many agencies for research and policy analysis institutions and units in education and related social sciences, and for networks of such agencies such as REDUC. However, such support has been a very small proportion of all international educational cooperation, and has typically responded more to the "regional" or "world-wide" priorities of donor agencies, such that kinds of knowledge seen locally as very relevant are often not developed. Moreover, large and powerful donor agencies still often routinely produce "regional" policy papers and directives which, while sometimes paying lip-service to intra-regional variation and the need for local knowledge, serve as multinational "cookbooks." A "one size fits all" approach to educational reform is nearly a guarantee of failure. This paper does not attempt to provide a single "recipe." Rather it provides a kind of taxonomy of elements and factors to take into account when thinking about educational reform and the role of international cooperation.

The discussion which follows is organized under six stages of the "policy cycle" as portrayed in figure 1. This is an old, oversimplified, but still useful device for organizing a potentially confusing array of issues. Each stage will be briefly identified, and then considered in greater detail. These stages pertain to policy development and implementation in all areas of government concern, but the discussion here will of course focus specifically on education.

Problem Formation: accurately assessing the current condition of the educational system, and its likely future state if current policies and practices continue, and reaching agreement among key policy actors and stakeholder groups as to which of these "conditions" represent "problems" which can and should be addressed by new policy or policy changes.

Policy Agenda: getting the identified policy problems high enough up on the government's policy agenda that, within some reasonable time frame, they will actually be addressed by government.

Policy Formulation: determining which of an array of potential "solutions" to the policy problems are most likely to be feasible and effective.

Policy Adoption: getting the proposed solutions formally "enacted" through whatever decision-making mechanisms are necessary and appropriate.

Policy Implementation: getting the enacted policy solutions actually operating effectively and more or less as intended in the myriad educational institutions of the nation.

Policy Evaluation: determining the impact of the implemented policies upon the performance of the educational system, identifying the sources of failure where it has occurred, and on the basis of that determination making such alterations as may be required.

In developing a long-term strategy for educational reform every one of these stages must be considered, and none can be taken for granted. Reform ideas and programs can go wrong, and have gone wrong, at each stage. Successfully passing through any one stage indicates nothing automatically about the probability of passing successfully through the next. Different sets of knowledge, skills, and strategies are normally required at each successive stage, usually requiring at least slightly different sets of people to be involved. Throughout, the process and the problems are much more "political" than "technical," having much more to do with conflicting human perceptions, ideologies, self- and group-interests, and emotions and values than with "hard" research data. This is true at each stage, including those which are often seen to be predominantly subject to technical analysis. One of the most common errors in planning educational reforms is to define the exercise in terms of, and concentrate exclusively upon, the technical aspects of policy formulation, implementation and (sometimes) evaluation. This has been particularly common in reform programs assisted by international donor agencies. Indeed, one of the most common sources of tension in international educational cooperation programs is disputes between donor agency officials who take a highly "technical" view and recipient nation officials who have a more "political" understanding. (See Samoff 1993, for a good account of this tension with reference to Africa. His analysis matches my own experience in Latin America.) Failure to take into account the political aspects of the three stages noted immediately above, or ignoring the stages of problem formation, policy agenda and policy adoption, are an almost sure recipe for failure. Unfortunately the most widely available "data" refer precisely to the technical side of formulation, implementation and evaluation. Much less has been published regarding the political aspects of reform planning, although the relatively few studies which are available indicate clearly their central importance (see Farrell 1986; Farrell 1990; Farrell, in press; Klees 1989; McGinn, Schiefelbein and Warwick 1979; McGinn and Street 1986; Schiefelbein 1975; Weiler 1988). Here one must rely heavily on the "lore" referred to above.

As with any model, this one is a necessary oversimplification of a much more complex reality. What are depicted here as separate stages often blend together, overlap chronologically or run in parallel. Using the stages as reference points is simply meant to ensure that none of the necessary sequences of activities in the long process which moves one from a sense that a problem exists to a solution implemented well and widely is overlooked. It will also be noted that the treatments below of the various stages differ in length. This does not indicate that some are more important than others, but rather that more information and experience are available about some than others.

Problem Formation

This initial stage is sometimes referred to as the process of converting "tolerable ironies" into policy problems. In any national educational system, however rich or poor the nation, there will always be a variety of "conditions" which are understood by at least some individuals or groups to be "problems" which should be addressed by policy. In many poor nations a very serious difficulty at this stage is the lack of reasonably accurate basic data regarding the status and performance of the system. In such cases a first task is establishing systems for collecting and analyzing such data. As noted above, in many Latin American nations international cooperation has been very helpful in creating the infrastructure for collecting and analyzing such basic data, although in many nations much remains to be done (Puryear 1993).

A common error, however, and this is particularly common among international agency officials, is assuming that once such an information system has been established (whether a simple data assembly unit in a Ministry of Education or a complex research establishment) problem identification becomes a more or less automatic technical matter. This is far from the case, as different individuals and groups can be expected to interpret the same "evidence" differently with respect to whether or not it represents an educational "policy problem," and if so, what sort of problem it represents. For example, a relatively high rate of unemployment among school leavers may be interpreted by some as an educational problem, by others as a problem of the economy about which education policy can do very little, and by others as a transient situation which will soon take care of itself. A given percentage of dropouts and/or repeaters within the schooling system may be considered by some as a serious problem within the educational system, by others as a normal and inevitable phenomenon (a routine consequence of differences in academic ability and necessary for the efficient streaming of youth into occupational categories for which they are most suited), and by still others as a product of an inequitable class system in the society about which schools can do little or nothing. Claims by employers and university professors that "standards" are declining may be roundly denied by teachers and students. "Hard" evidence from national or international testing programs that average scores are declining will be interpreted by some as a clear indication that the quality of the school system is deteriorating, but by others as evidence that the system is succeeding in holding more lower ability and/or lower class students in school longer.

These differing interpretations of the "evidence" reflect differing ideological assumptions, differing assumptions about what is "normal," and usually differing patterns of self- and group-interest. That is, they are not typically or simply "technical" disputes, but are deeply and intensely political, and must be dealt with as such. Moreover, even if one can achieve a reasonably broad agreement that a given set of "conditions" represent a set of policy problems, there may be considerable disagreement about the relative priority among them. It is also common for there to be serious disagreements at this stage between individuals within a country and representatives of international donor agencies, who come in with their own perceptions and their agencies' priorities. Resolving disagreements at this first stage is frequently one of the most difficult and sensitive tasks in the reform process, and one of the most time-consuming. It is also a stage where disagreements are frequently assumed away, by educators or researchers within the country who believe that they, with their expertise, "know" what the problems and priorities are, or by foreign agency officials who come with their own agencies' priorities and cannot imagine serious and legitimate disagreement, or by "expert consultants" who often bring their own preconceptions with them (e.g., if you bring in a computer or distance education expert, you are likely to be told that you have a serious computer or distance education problem—this is the adult equivalent of the "Law of the Hammer": give a four-year-old a hammer and suddenly everything will need hammering). If such inevitable disagreements regarding which "conditions" constitute "policy problems," and which problems are most important, are not resolved at the outset, at least to the point where most key actors and stakeholder groups agree, the probability of carrying the change process through to conclusion is low.

Policy Agenda

Even under the best of circumstances governments face far more demands upon their resources (money, energy, time) than can possibly be accommodated. Budgets are tight, senior and middle level officials face overcrowded schedules, legislative agendas and cabinet meeting agendas are full to overflowing (in one government with which I have worked—a reasonably typical case in my experience—the general understanding among senior government officials is that except in a crisis one can get discussion of any particular policy issue on cabinet agenda no more than once a year, if lucky). Almost all, if not all, other ministries are competing for government attention to policy problems they regard as being as important as, if not more important than, educational policy problems. Even if there has been some formal statement from government about being committed to "do something" about educational policy problems, it cannot be assumed that this will translate into high interest *at a particular point in time* in the particular set of prioritized issues arising from the policy formation stage within the education sector. The strategies most appropriate to move a set of educational problems sufficiently high on a government's overall policy agenda to insure that effort will be exerted to "do something" about them will vary enormously from nation to nation, and over time within a given nation, depending upon, among other things, the relative political strength of various key political actors at any point in time. With regard to these judgments local knowledge must be decisive. International cooperation can have little if any constructive force at this stage, except by slowly altering the general international "climate of opinion" to which large numbers of key political actors in any given nation respond. (See Grindle 1989, for a useful discussion of the importance of the perceptual frames and assumptions of "policy elites.") Unesco's *Major Project in the Field of Education in the Latin American and Caribbean Region*, and the dialogue before, during and after the *World Conference on Education for All* are good examples of this indirect effect of international cooperation on political agenda-setting. But *direct* attempts by officials of international agencies to alter the policy agenda in a particular nation in the (false) name of international cooperation are almost always bound to be counterproductive, unless they happen to coincide with the efforts of strategically placed, locally knowledgeable and highly skilled local political actors. Unfortunately, a current trend in many international cooperation agencies in the Americas is precisely to try to influence the policy agenda of other nations directly; for example, by making balance of payment or structural adjustment supports contingent upon particular policy (in our case, *educational* policy) directions. This trend is more powerful in other "developing" regions than in the Americas (it is for example blatant in Africa under the rubric of "Structural Adjustment Policies"), but it is still worrisome in our region. *Fiscal blackmail is not a sound ground upon which to base educational reform.* Officials from international cooperation agencies based in rich nations should learn from their own national experiences. There are myriad examples in "developed" nations of educational reform initiatives from educational "experts" languishing because of inability to get through the policy agenda stage. If influencing educational, and national, policy agendas is very difficult to do from inside, it is even more difficult to do from outside. Working toward building up an international climate of opinion regarding priorities in educational policy is in the long term (and all educational change of importance is long term) the only effective strategy for international cooperation.

Policy Formulation

Work on this stage, judging which "solutions" to identified policy problems are most likely to be effective (and cost-effective), often overlaps chronologically with the previous stage. Indeed, the knowledge that there is a potentially feasible and effective solution to a policy problem can raise that problem to a prominent place on a government's policy agenda. (On this "legitimation theory" view see Weiler 1983 and Fuller 1991). It is with reference to this question, what "works," that most of the "hard" evidence is found. Much of that evidence has been analyzed and summarized in a series of "state of the art" papers, usually financed by or directly produced by large donor agencies, particularly the World Bank. (See, e.g., Heyneman, Farrell, and Sepulveda 1978; Fuller 1986; Lockheed and Verspoor 1990; Farrell and Heyneman 1991; Farrell and Oliveira 1993; plus many Latin American regional summaries produced by institutions associated with the LARRAG and REDUC networks.) The major conclusions coming from that literature are generally well known and will not be reviewed here. Rather, some cautionary notes will be provided. First, there have been strong methodological critiques advanced regarding many of the underlying research studies, claiming for example that the regression techniques used in many of the investigations produce highly unstable and misleading results (Klees 1989), or that the statistical model used in most education-labor market studies produces results which are inherently uninterpretable (Farrell and Schiefelbein 1985). These problems can be taken into account when carefully reading the *individual* studies, but are very difficult to deal with when many such studies are summarized.

It should also be noted that while the amount of evidence regarding particular schooling factors that affect educational or labor market achievement in Latin America has been increasing rapidly in recent years, the total amount available is far less than in the United States and Canada. On questions where there may be hundreds of studies in North America, there may be none, or only a few, from all of Latin America. It is also clear now that educational research results from North America cannot be automatically transferred to Latin America. The available evidence is also spotty. Some questions have received much attention, others little. Some sub-regions or individual nations have produced much more educational research than others. Much of the research that has been done is still not readily accessible, although the REDUC network has made strong gains in this area. Moreover, the investigations themselves are of several different types. Some are large-scale correlational exercises, others are small-scale experimental studies, still others are evaluations of a particular program or policy in a particular nation. This makes it difficult to adequately summarize the results. And qualitative research, which often provides strong insights into "what works," why and how, is rarely included in summaries (for an exception see Fuller 1991).

Finally, just as we cannot assume that research results from North America will necessarily translate to Latin America, we also cannot assume that research results from any particular cultural group within Latin America are generalizable to other cultural groups. This is particularly important when considering educational policy for indigenous peoples. The anthropological evidence (see Hall 1985) is now clear that children from different cultures "learn to learn" differently. What will "work" educationally for children or adults from one culture may be quite ineffective or counter-productive in others. What all of this suggests is that any conclusions drawn from the available evidence must be cautious and tentative, and as location-specific as possible. I have suggested elsewhere that the best way to approach the general research evidence when considering educational policy in any particular nation is to consider it as simply providing some hints or suggestions regarding what directions may be "best bets," "worst bets," and "promising possibilities" (Farrell 1989b).

Unfortunately, there is a tendency, which appears to be increasing, for officials of donor agencies, in a "search for certitude," to take the results of regional or international "state of the art" papers as "gospel," and attempt to apply them willy-nilly to all nations in a region, particularly where there is not a strong local research base. This is particularly true of the World Bank (Samoff 1993), although there certainly are exceptions (its support of *Escuela Nueva* in Colombia and MECE in Chile appears to have responded to local research results). The way in which USAID has been responding to the results of large-scale research/summary exercises it has sponsored, such as BRIDGES, appears to have much the same character, in spite of appropriate cautions from the researchers involved. My own observation of "policy dialogue" within Canadian CIDA finds much the same search for certainty, and over-generalization. This is an extremely worrisome tendency, and is to be avoided and resisted if locally sensible "policy solutions" are to be formulated.

There is another problem with the "what works" research, and the way in which it is often used in policy discussions/negotiations between donor agencies and recipient nations. It generally assumes the existence of, and works within (to strengthen some elements of), the "standard technology of schooling." That standard technology, or standard delivery system, normally has the following elements (and comparative research has shown a steady worldwide convergence toward this model over the past decades):

1. One hundred to several hundred children/youth assembled (sometimes compulsorily) in a building called a school;
2. For three to six hour per day, where;
3. They are divided into groups of 20 to 60;
4. To work with a single adult (a "certified" teacher) in a single room;
5. For (especially at the upper levels) discrete periods of 40 to 60 minutes, each devoted to a separate "subject," with;
6. Supporting learning materials, e.g., books, chalkboards, notebooks, workbooks and worksheets (and in technical areas laboratories, workbenches, practice sites, etc.), all of which is organized by;
7. A standard curriculum, set by an authority level much above the individual school, normally the central or provincial/state government, which all are expected to "cover."
8. Adults "teach" and students "receive instruction" from them.
9. Teachers (and/or a central exam system) "evaluate" student learning and provide recognized formal certificates for "passing" particular "grades" or "levels."
10. Most or all of the financial support comes from national or regional governments, or other kinds of authority (e.g., in church-related schools) well above the local community.

There are a variety of explanations (or "theories") regarding why and how this particular way of delivering opportunities to learn on a large scale has become well-nigh universal (see Fuller 1991 for a useful summary). However, a careful examination of the cross-national literature from anthropology (Hall 1985) and learning psychology (see Case 1985 re: children, and Kidd 1973 and Knowles 1983 re: adults) regarding how young people and adults best learn suggests that this "standard technology" is inherently ineffective and inefficient. People of whatever age simply do not learn best under these arrangements. I have argued elsewhere that one of the problems with using the "what works," or "school effectiveness," literature to devise educational policy is that we are, particularly in richer nations, reaching the limits of the already limited effectiveness and efficiency of that standard model (Farrell 1989b). However, on a more hopeful note, throughout Latin America (and North America and the rest of the world) one finds small and large attempts to fundamentally alter this traditional model, using combinations of fully trained teachers, partially trained teachers, para-teachers, community resource people, radio, correspondence lessons, peer tutoring, student constructed learning materials, students flowing freely between the "school" and the community, often with local financing, or with alterations in the cycle of the school "day" or the school "year." Such change programs do not simply alter one feature of the standard school (e.g., change one part of the curriculum) or strengthen one or several parts of the standard model (e.g., add more textbooks or improve teacher training), or add one or two new features. Rather, they represent a thorough reorganization of the standard technology of schooling such that the learning program, although often occurring in or based in a building called a "school," is quite different from what one normally expects to be happening in a school. They tend to break down the boundaries between "formal" and "nonformal" education, and tend to focus less on "teaching" and more on "learning." Where they have been evaluated the results generally have been very positive. New groups of learners are successfully reached, and learning results are at least as good as, if not better than, those obtained in standard schools, and the costs are typically no more than, if not less than, those of the standard model. Thus, from a cost-effectiveness point of view they are generally very successful. Moreover, because they typically serve the most marginalized, hardest to reach and hardest to teach (in the standard mode) students, the learning results from a "value added" perspective are quite spectacular (Schiefelbein 1991; Psacharopolous, Rojas and Velez 1993).

Two outstanding examples of such "model breaking" educational reform programs in Latin America are the *Escuela Nueva* program in Colombia (Schiefelbein 1991) and various vocational training (or education for production) training programs for disadvantaged youth who have been very poorly served by the standard schooling system (Corvalan-Vasquez 1988). International cooperation, through a variety of donor agencies, has been key to the development of both of these alternative programs from initial ideas and small-scale experimentation to large scale successful implementation. Although these are success stories, international support for such model-breaking programs is, unfortunately, rather rare. As noted above, one can find throughout Latin America many such potentially promising educational change programs, often developed by local teachers or risk-taking action/researchers in response to the desperate situations they routinely encounter; but most are unknown by Ministry of Education officials (standard procedures and reporting channels tend to shut such information out), let alone by international agency officials who work only with government officials, although knowledge about them is often common currency among NGOs and local teachers and base level administrators. A very useful role for international cooperation would be to assist in identifying such potentially useful fundamental alterations in the standard model of schooling, funding detailed small-scale studies of how they got started, and how they work and achieve their results, and supporting carefully evaluated experiments in diffusing them to other locations. Such work can be highly productive in the long term, as the two examples noted above illustrate, but it is not typically attempted by donor agencies, principally, it seems to me, because the support required is too small scale, risky, and long term to fit well within the normal administrative practices of such agencies. Nonetheless, a potentially very creative role of international cooperation would be to fund a set of locally based and locally administered micro-regional programs for identification and experimentation with such locally and independently developed fundamental innovations. If such support were linked with support for regional research and information dissemination networks such as REDUC, the potential for maximizing the influence of such knowledge as is already locally available would be high. It appears to be very difficult for international cooperation agencies to play this kind of role, but the two examples noted above indicate that it is not impossible. Detailed examination of how these successes occurred would be very helpful.

Policy Adoption

Getting a set of policy problems high on a government agenda, and *keeping them there* (often a very difficult matter), and arriving at a set of reform propositions which are analytically sound and generally supported by stakeholder groups, is no guarantee that government will *actually do anything about them.* The previous stages require a combination of analytical and political skill. At this stage the job is almost wholly political, and can be accomplished only by individuals who are highly skilled, locally based and locally knowledgeable political operatives (whatever their formal job descriptions might be). It is at this stage that the competitive and conflicting interests of other ministries and agencies of government come most strongly into play, and convincing the Finance Minister (or his/her officials) becomes crucial (unless one is in the rare and happy position of advocating a reform proposition which will not increase the total budgetary allocation to education). Very carefully done cost analysis is often necessary to convince finance ministry officials, and it is frequently useful to be able to demonstrate that a significant portion of the costs of the reform program will be supported by reallocations within the existing Ministry of Education budget. The very "fuzzy" nature of the boundaries between education and other social policy sectors can often be used to turn potential opponents from other ministries or agencies into allies, by incorporating some of their goals and interests into the educational reform proposal (this is often done at the policy formulation stage). One must beware, however, of creating "smorgasbord" or "Christmas tree" programs, which consist of large numbers of only vaguely related elements. Such projects often result from a confluence of local political need to satisfy a variety of competing interests, and the desire of donor agencies to put together an administratively convenient (i.e., large enough) investment package. Such reform projects are generally cost-inefficient and very difficult to implement and administer effectively, and should be avoided.

Enactment of an educational reform package typically requires an array of decisions (legislation, directives, decrees, regulations), many of which are obvious but others less so. For example, reform programs have sometimes been blocked or seriously slowed because necessary changes in, or exceptions to, import taxes or restrictions could not be obtained and essential material could not be acquired, or because necessary personnel changes were blocked by existing civil service rules which were not changed. Thus, to successfully enact the reform, someone, or some group, has to know clearly which parts of the overall reform proposal have to be approved and enacted by which agencies or institutions of government, and through which processes, and keep track of who is responsible for which parts of the overall process, keeping everything running more or less in parallel. It is not uncommon to find a reform scheme stymied because while almost all of its necessary elements have been "approved" one key element is irretrievably stuck in some bureaucratic or political swamp. (In my experience this is as common in rich nations as in poor ones.) If there are active opponents to the reform proposal one must assume that they will be looking for precisely such "sticking points" as strategic areas to exert blockage power. Outside consultants or international agency officials can often play a useful role here in asking the right questions (of the "What has to be done here?" or "Are there any regulations which need changing there?" sort), but they can never presume to have the right answers.

As in all political decision making, judgments regarding proper "timing" are crucial; in all political systems there are good times and bad times for attempting to enact policy changes, and these follow a pattern which has little or nothing to do with the internal cycles and needs of the educational system. These political cycles also have nothing particularly to do with the decision and funding cycles of donor agencies. Waiting until the "time is right" politically to maximize the chances of a reform proposal passing through the adoption phase is frequently very difficult for technically oriented planners/policy developers and international agency officials responding to their own bureaucratic constraints, but it is essential. In contrast, it sometimes happens that the politically propitious moment for enactment occurs before all of the technical work has been completed. In such cases it is usually far better to take advantage of the political opportunity, as it is generally easier and quicker to fill in technical gaps later than it is to wait for or try to recreate the political moment. Indeed, being ready to move when political windows of opportunity open up (usually briefly) is a key element of reform design and delivery. Another key aspect of the "timing" question is deciding whether to attempt to enact the entire reform package all at once, or to proceed by stages. There is no universal prescription. Both options have sometimes succeeded and sometimes failed.

To repeat, dealing effectively with all of the issues noted in this section depends upon locally based, knowledgeable and sensitive political judgment. This cannot be emphasized too much. Political misjudgment during the policy adoption phase is an extremely frequent cause of educational reform failure, in both rich and poor nations. In developing nations such misjudgments are often, unfortunately, the result of pressure from outside consultants or international agency officials who are insufficiently knowledgeable about and sensitive to the needs and constraints of local political decision makers, and the way in which politics "works" in a particular nation, and who are responding primarily to the decision cycles of their own agencies and their own career-advancement imperative to "move the money." It should be noted finally that while reliance on such local knowledge and judgment is essential, it is no guarantee that a reform proposal will successfully work its way through the policy adoption phase. Political judgment is inherently risky and failure-prone, as any number of involuntarily retired politicians can tell us. But not relying on such local knowledge is a near guarantee of failure.

Implementation

Managing the *implementation* of change in educational organizations is more complex than in most other public or private enterprises. In education one is attempting to deliver (or change the delivery of) an intangible end-product (learning) on a non-sale basis to a diverse, diffuse, and often reluctant clientele, using delivery agents (teachers) over whose routine daily behavior one has minimum or no effective control, and in conditions where efforts to exert such control are frequently counter productive to the general goals of the system. Beyond this, in educational change one is dealing with what is most important to most people in a society: the destiny of their children and the future of the society in which their, and everyone else's, children will live their adult lives. Almost every group in a society are potential stakeholders in the process, passions are easily and quickly aroused, and the deepest value conflicts in a society are played out in debates over, and reactions to, attempts at educational reform (Farrell 1990). These passions are found throughout the policy cycle, but they come very quickly to the fore during the implementation stage. For here, abstract notions and vague possibilities begin to assume a reality in the lives of youngsters. It is at this stage that *potential* stakeholders tend to become *real* stakeholders. If their interests have not been taken into account fully throughout the process, they will make them fully visible here. The management of educational reform implementation is *quintessentially political*. It is not fundamentally a technical exercise is which PERT charts, logical framework analyses, organizational analyses, or other tools of the professional "change agent" trade, which are very much in vogue in donor agencies, have much use (except as ways to keep files straight and an office efficiently running). The single most common cause of implementation failure is focusing on the technical and forgetting the political; of forgetting that implementation means changing the routine behavior of very large numbers of people at all levels of the system (including students and their parents) who cannot effectively be "commanded." It is a matter of treating people honestly rather than manipulatively, of persuasion, demonstration, tolerance for variation, and getting the positive incentives right.

It is extremely important to build in a capacity to learn *during* implementation. Things will always turn out differently than expected in at least some important areas. Educational systems are *systems*. Changing anything will change other things in ways which are almost impossible to fully anticipate. Ongoing learning capacity also allows detection of blockage points early enough to do something effective about them. Ongoing "evaluation" (see below) provides the "data" for such learning capacity, but equally important is keeping administrative systems flexible enough and regulations general enough that changes can easily be made as required in response to such data. Rigid bureaucratic rules and complex and time-consuming processes for approval of changes in a program design imposed by international donor agencies are a major inhibitor to the development of this ongoing learning capacity.

Top-down, centrally driven, and command-oriented forms of implementation almost never work well; and where they can be *made* to work well they tend to create resentments and resistances which make future changes even more difficult and impair the ongoing learning capacity discussed above. Several of the most commonly cited implementation "models" in the literature (e.g., Fullan 1982; Miles 1987) can best be described as "disguised" or "manipulative" top-down models. They are in essence approaches for manipulating teachers and lower level administrators so that they will behave in accordance with the ideas or decrees of senior officials or "experts." Teachers are considered as "objects" whose behavior is to be modified, not as sources of knowledge, insight, information and ideas. Parents and students hardly figure at all in such models. By manipulating or ignoring precisely those groups whose enthusiastic collaboration is essential to the solid implementation of significant educational reform, such models are recipes for serious problems in the mid- to long-term. Teachers must have the opportunity to learn: about the proposed reform and about how to operate it successfully in their own classrooms. (This assumes that their views have been given significant weight during the policy formulation process. If not, there is little that can be done at this stage to correct for the error; the reform effort will be doomed to serious implementation problems.) This teacher learning is best conceived and arranged not as a "teaching" process (experts from the ministry or the university going out to tell the teachers) but as the provision of opportunities to learn, through teacher centers, demonstration classes and centers, chances to experiment safely, mentoring arrangements, and such. This kind of *innovation diffusion* approach to implementation often appears to work more slowly than a major-push, centrally-driven "blitz." But in the medium to long term it tends to work far better and deeper. Unfortunately, the "limited term project" mentality common in donor agencies works directly against such a long-term diffusion approach to implementation.

Evaluation

There is vast and generally well-known technical/methodological literature on "evaluation" which there is no need to recapitulate here.

Rather, a few points which are sometimes overlooked in the literature and practice will be briefly noted.

Much of the data required for routine ongoing evaluation of a reform program are available from information collected by the Ministry of Education (and other agencies of government) for routine administration purposes (e.g., enrollment patterns, test scores, assigned grades, financial flows, and the like). However, such data are often incomplete and/or wildly inaccurate, and are often hidden or purposely distorted for bureaucratic or political reasons. Finding out where the good data are before mounting a major reform effort is often an expensive but essential up-front investment. Moreover, even the good data can easily get lost in bureaucratic files if special systems are not established to ensure that they arrive in a timely fashion on the desks of those responsible for monitoring the reform project. One cannot simply assume that because such data exist somewhere in the ministry (or other clements of government) they will automatically be provided to those who need them for project evaluation purposes. Since the possession and control of information is a major source of power, it is safer to assume the contrary, and therefore to establish special procedures for rechanneling such data. Funding research/policy analysis institutions outside government, or at least outside normal bureaucratic channels, which can provide a relatively independent view of such data could be a very useful role for international cooperation. Many of the institutions associated with the REDUC network, supported by a variety of donor agencies, have played a very useful role in this regard.

Non-routine evaluation exercises involve the *creation* of information not normally produced from the ordinary functioning of the educational system. They are often essential, but they are also expensive. Because of the cost it is important that such exercises be carefully and judiciously designed, taking into account information that is already available somewhere in the system, and the use to which each piece of newly created information will be put. Two of the most common and costly errors in reform evaluation design (and I have seen these repeatedly in international cooperation projects, usually because international agency officials were following some sort of agency "cookbook") are (1) collecting information which is already available somewhere in the system and (2) collecting information which is never used.

A mix of evaluation techniques and approaches is required for most reform projects, since they combine a variety of objectives and processes. Both quantitative and qualitative "evaluation research" approaches are usually needed. Often, the most generally useful sources of information are classroom observations, and the opinions and experiences of students, teachers, and parents. Much of this information is anecdotal; setting up systems for recording and archiving such anecdotal evidence is usually well worth the investment. Although the pattern is slowly changing, it is still the case that large international donor agencies rely upon and take seriously only "hard" quantitative evaluation data. (Samoff 1993, provides a very good analysis of the organizational dynamics behind this quantitative data focus regarding the World Bank's work in Africa, which is generalizable to many other agencies and the Americas.)

Evaluation exercises, especially "end of project" evaluations, designed and/or commissioned by funding agencies are often quite useless from the point of view of the recipient country, as they focus heavily on the administrative requirements of the donor (e.g., was the money disbursed on schedule, did planned activities take place on time, has material been acquired and disbursed on schedule, etc.) rather than on actual ground-level changes and the results of the reform.

Roles of Donor Agencies

From the above it should be evident that serious educational reform, of the sort that seems to be needed *throughout* the Americas (and not just in Latin America), is a slow, complex, chancy and highly political business. A central argument here is that many of the standard operating procedures of international donor agencies, who are the major financiers of international educational cooperation within the Americas, and thus the central actors in the process, run directly counter to, and interfere with, the way in which effective major educational change takes place, in the relatively rare occasions in which it does take place. Many of these patterns of behavior have been noted briefly in the pages above. Some of the more important are listed below, in summary fashion.

There is a tendency among donor agencies to overgeneralize from the results of often problematic research and attempt to apply "standard solutions" to all nations in a region. This is combined with a pattern of "faddishness" as different sets of standard solutions go in and out of fashion. For example, support for secondary level technical or "diversified" education was once very much "in"; now it is less so. Support for primary education was long a low priority; lately it has become fashionable.

There is within donor agencies a predominant "search for certitude" and a desire for "quick fixes" which ignore just how risky and slow effective educational change usually is.

There is an overwhelming tendency to regard educational change as a "technical" matter and to consider "politics" as at best a bothersome nuisance. The prevailing view is captured in the following quote: "The politicization of decision-making in Latin America has traditionally undermined the role of technical analysis" (Reimers 1991, 348). To imagine that politically sensitive educational decisions (and they are almost all such) could be taken without "politicization" is destructively unrealistic. If "political factors" are taken into account at all they are typically viewed as something to be gotten around or gotten through rather than as an inherent and essential part of the change process.

Funding patterns are normally short term compared to the length of time required for educational change, and based on one or a collection of specific projects with rigid (as well as too short) time lines. *Educational systems do not change that way.* When reasonably long-term funding has been arranged, usually through a succession of short-term projects, and some success has been achieved, this is frequently a signal to the donor to cut off the funding and redirect the resources to some area of more "desperate" need. This cuts off the possibility of the really important benefits which only come in the more long term, and effectively penalizes the recipients for having been successful.

The administrative imperative to work with large investment packages (keeping the donor's administrative costs down) produces "smorgasbord" or "Christmas tree" programs consisting of collections of discrete projects which are fundamentally unrelated (except perhaps in the prose of a proposal writer with high creative writing skills).

Constant personnel changes in donor agencies produce serious continuity and institutional memory problems in necessarily long-term programs. This happens regularly even with relatively short-term projects. I was recently involved in a three-year project of quite small scale which experienced four changes of donor agency program officers. Much of our time was spent (wasted) in bringing each successive agency official "up to speed." This is not, I am sure, what the taxpayers of Canada imagined they were financing when their members of parliament supported the overseas assistance appropriation. Recipient country project managers have to spend an inordinate amount of their time educating successive waves of equally uninformed donor agency officials. (As one such official said to me in exasperation a few years ago: "The least they could do is talk to each other while they play musical chairs!") This pattern may be great for the personal growth and career advancement of donor agency officials, but it doesn't do much for educational reform.

Donor agencies funding or looking for projects in education in a particular nation rarely work effectively together, and seldom have a clear idea of what everyone else is doing. Their competitive, jealous, non-cooperative collective presence in a particular nation makes educational reform even harder than it normally is. Indeed, one frequently sees the bizarre situation in which the donors are even more uncooperative among themselves (and more assiduously protective of their own national interests) than are the recipients who are accused by the donors of being overly protective of their national interests. One might call the situation Kafkaesque, but that would be unfair to Kafka. He never described a situation quite so strange.

In one sense the obvious "lesson" is that donor agencies should alter the behaviors noted above. I must admit, however, that I have no clear idea as to how that might actually come about. Some would argue that these patterns of behavior are the inevitable consequence of well-nigh universal organizational imperatives of large bureaucracies, and therefore nearly impossible to change so long as international cooperation is financed and administered by large bureaucratic organizations. Others would argue that they are the ineluctable consequence of highly unequal power relationships between donor and recipient nations, and will not change until those power relationships change. I am convinced of one thing, however. If these patterns of behavior and attitude are not changed the probability is very low that international cooperation can in general promote and support educational reform in the Americas; indeed, if such patterns are not changed the probability is highest that international cooperation will be a *hindrance* to educational reform. It will most likely be time, energy and money not only wasted, but used counterproductively. There are, however, some "successes;" cases in which significant educational reform has been accomplished, and in which international cooperation has played an important role. Cases which come to mind and with which I am personally familiar include the educational reform in Chile during the Frei regime, the development of the REDUC network, the development of education for production programs for disadvantaged youth, the *Escuela Nueva* program in Colombia, and (as far as one can tell at the moment), the MECE project in Chile. My own impression, based on personal experience, and the "lore" referred to above, is that these successes have occurred because the local change agents were smart enough and lucky enough to circumvent or overcome the donor agency patterns discussed above, and/or were able to manipulate the donor agencies to their own advantage. A very useful role for the Inter-American Dialogue would be to *initiate a careful investigation of how these "successes" occurred and how international cooperation was in these cases actually helpful, and to compare these cases to a good sample of the more typical failures in educational reform and international cooperation in support of it.* A further useful role would be to *facilitate discussions with donor agencies regarding ways to alter the counterproductive behaviors discussed above.*

Toward a Different Model of International Cooperation

Underlying the organizational behavior difficulties discussed above is a deeper problem which has been briefly alluded to. The basic "model" of international cooperation which has become well-nigh universal is not the "solution" but the "problem." That model, the "foreign aid" or "technical assistance" model, is inherently hierarchical; one set of nations (the "donors") bring their resources and expertise to bear upon the problems of another set of nations (the "recipients"). It is assumed implicitly (and sometimes explicitly), that the recipients have the "problems" and the donors have the "solutions" and the resources required to apply them. It is assumed, although this is rarely said out loud and often officially denied, that there is a natural confluence between having more resources (money) and having better ideas or more "expertise." Even when "ideas" from recipient nations are financed by donor agencies, those ideas must first be accepted and approved by those with the funds. Such a model necessarily breeds arrogance on one side and resentment and frustration on the other; and it has in general proven to be ineffective or counterproductive in promoting educational reform in the Americas. I argue that even where it has in a general sense *seemed* to be successful it has sown the seeds of its own failure. In pursuing this argument it is useful to separate discussion of fiscal flows and ideational flows.

Fiscal Flows

It is obviously the case that one of the differences between rich nations and poor nations is that the former have more money than the latter. It is also obviously the case that at least some of the educational reform problems in poor nations cannot be dealt with without infusions of money from richer nations. But *how* such money gets transferred is all important, and the record within the Americas over the past few decades has not been encouraging. Reimer's analysis of fiscal flows in support of international cooperation in education within the Americas over the past decades is most instructive. He notes that the massive educational expansion in Latin America during the 1970s was "credit led" (Reimers 1990, 45). That is, a significant portion of the *marginal* costs required by that expansion were financed by borrowing from international donors. However, the educational borrowings were part of the overall debt whose servicing created the "debt crisis" of the 1980s and 90s, whose effect has been (among many other things) to cripple the educational systems of many Latin American nations and to, in effect, bring them back to where they were, or worse than they were, before the expansion of the 1970s. In sum, international debt-financed educational change helped create the cause of its own destruction (Reimers 1991). This is not to argue for a cessation of transfers of funds from those who have more money than they need to those who have less than they need. It *is* to argue for an alteration of the *terms* of such transfers so that they do not create a repetition of that disastrous cycle.

Ideational Flows

The notion that educational "ideas" or "solutions" originating in the North of the Americas are better or more powerful than those originating in the South of the Americas is bizarre and arrogant, and indicates that educational "experts" from the North have little understanding of just how badly they have managed collectively to diagnose and correct the difficulties in their own educational systems. The operative phrase here should be: "Physician, heal thyself!" The educational research and reform industry in the United States and Canada is massive, offering gainful employment to thousands of professors, researchers, and change agents. Yet complaints of massive educational problems are common currency in both of these rich societies, and their educational systems seem to have remained impervious to the expenditures of huge sums of money on their putative improvement.

Fierce scholarly and political debates rage in both nations regarding the causes of the educational malaise, and what might be done about it. Attendance at any annual meeting of the American Educational Research Association or the Canadian Society for the Study of Education, or organizations of various specialized groups of practitioners or researchers, will bear witness to this rampant confusion and disagreement. Yet, leading "experts" from both of these rich American nations regularly presume to tell educational officials from the poorer nations of our hemisphere what *they* ought to do about *their* educational problems! The educational and economic/political disadvantages of members of racial and ethnic minorities in both Canada and the United States continue, in general, to remain impervious to attempts at educational reform. The economies of both nations are mired in deep recession, and various attempts at educational change and job training schemes have had nil effect to date. In both nations income distribution has been steadily worsening since the early 1980s. What exactly do either of these nations have to teach to the rest of the hemisphere about how to use educational reform to improve either economic growth or social equity? My answer is simple: practically nothing at all, except as salutary bad examples. But of course it would be very hard to even imagine a well-paid, upper-middle class professional representative of one of the donor agencies (or even a middle-middle class representative of one of the increasingly noticeable nongovernmental agencies) actually admitting that they don't really know what to do; that in reality nobody knows what to do. It would be even harder for them to admit that indeed the primary beneficiaries of the "foreign aid" model of international cooperation have been the quite well paid professional administrators of those otherwise often useless, and frequently counterproductive, North to South fiscal flows.

What has to be done is to recognize collectively that whether we speak English, Spanish or Portuguese, whether we are members of rich nations or poor nations, we are all equal in our befuddlement about what sorts of educational changes might contribute to the solution of the economic, social and political problems all nations of the Americas face, and about how to enact and implement effectively such educational reforms. At the same time, all nations of the hemisphere have examples of modest but potentially promising "successes." And we all are, or at least ought to be, equally puzzled by the direction and consequences of the evident massive and rapid changes in the global economic, political, social, environmental (and educational) conditions. In this context it is somewhat disheartening to note that all of the background documents referred to in the first paragraph of this paper are redolent with language which reflects the traditional "foreign aid" understanding of international cooperation. For example, in these documents the "problems" are all discussed in relation to Latin America, as though the social, economic, political and educational problems were not equally difficult and intractable in North America. But, if we were all collectively to admit to it in due intellectual humility, the collective and mutual confusion regarding the changing nature of our world, and the place of educational reform in dealing with it, could provide the basis for developing a quite different model of international cooperation. I have elsewhere referred to this model as "horizontal intellectual cooperation" and have described one small effort at enacting it among one Canadian and two Chilean educational research institutions (Farrell 1989; see also Shaeffer 1991). This model starts from the assumption that we *all* have much to teach each other and much to learn from each other; that all of our knowledge is equally tentative and equally valid; and that such knowledge derived from any given society or culture must be carefully tested and validated before being applied in any other society or culture. This model would place less emphasis on the transfer of funds among agencies and governments, and more on the collective creation and critical examination of *ideas*. Operationally, such a model would imply support for institutions and centers which create and analyze educational knowledge, and for collaborative interchange among them. Support for the expansion of networks such as REDUC would be a good place to start. Collective exploration of how this model of international educational cooperation might be enacted would be a task worthy of the Inter-American Dialogue. It would likely be a far better use of such resources as can be found than trying to "fine tune" the traditional "foreign aid" model of international cooperation.

Some Concluding Observations

The reader of these pages may arrive at this point with the conclusion that I take a pessimistic (perhaps unduly pessimistic) view of the possibilities of achieving needed educational changes, and of the possibilities of inventing modes of international cooperation which might support such change efforts. The experience, and analysis of it, briefly outlined above, could easily lead one to such a pessimistic conclusion, but that is not where I will end this essay. I actually take from this experience what might best be called a "cautiously optimistic" conclusion. It *is* clear that it is extremely difficult to successfully accomplish large-scale, national-level and top-down educational reform programs. But at the same time we have many examples of very successful change attempts at the level of the local school, or a small system of schools, and occasionally (as in Colombia's *Escuela Nueva* program) in systems of thousands of schools. That is, while it seems very difficult to change a *national school system*, it appears relatively easy to change *a classroom*, or, *a school*, in ways which are often unknown by national- or international-level officials. And thousands of such very local changes can, over time (in an innovation diffusion process), build from the bottom-up into a major change in the overall "national" education effort. What we have to do, I would suggest, is to identify these local successes and *learn from them*. That task is not to invent and implement "the innovation" or "the reform" across the whole national territory, but rather to develop and unleash a *capacity to innovate* throughout the system. The result would likely be a highly variegated, locally adapted, set of learning systems which, while occurring in buildings called "schools," would have few of the characteristics of the "standard model" of schooling outlined earlier.

It is not yet at all clear how that capacity to innovate which we see in these localized cases of successful change can be generalized. It does seem clear that, under the right circumstances, even very poorly paid teachers working under extremely difficult conditions, *can* enact major educational changes in their own classrooms and schools. It does seem clear that national educational system administrators *can*, under the right circumstances, become change agents rather than change blockers. It does seem clear that, under the right circumstances, officials of international donor agencies *can* work through or around the constraints of the bureaucratic systems in which they operate to assist in the creation of truly hopeful innovations. The periodic successes indicate that the task is possible. But how do we convert the *possible* into the *probable*? How do we create the "circumstances" which can unleash the human energy and sense of vocation which draw most people into the "education" and "development" fields in the first place? I do not claim in this paper to have provided many answers—certainly not any definitive answers—to that question. A central task of the Inter-American Dialogue would be to provide a forum in which the answer to that question can be collaboratively developed by people representing all of the groups which have a stake in the way in which their society manages the provision of opportunities for its citizens (young and old) to learn. But one cannot possibly get the "answer" right until one gets the "question" right. My main aim in this paper has been to contribute to getting the question right.

FIGURE 1
POLICY CYCLE

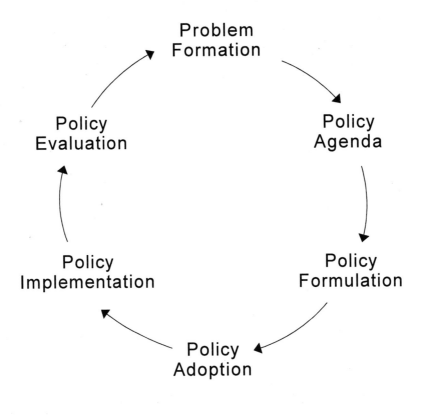

Source: Anderson, Brady and Bullock 1978.

BIBLIOGRAPHY

Anderson, J., D. Brady, and C. Bullock. 1978. *Public Policy and Politics in America*. Monterey, CA: Brooks/Cole Publishing Company.

Bailey, T. 1991. "Jobs of the Future and the Education They Will Require: Evidence from Occupational Forecasts." *Educational Researcher* 20.2: 11-20.

Bryson, J. 1988. *Strategic Planning for Public and Non-Profit Organizations*. San Francisco: Jossey Bass.

Caillods, F. 1989. *The Prospects for Educational Planning*. Paris: Unesco/International Institute for Educational Planning.

Case, R. 1985. *Intellectual Development: Birth to Adulthood*. Toronto: Academic Press.

COPS (Canadian Occupational Projection System). 1990. *Job Futures Volume 1. Occupational Futures. An Occupational Outlook to 1995. 1990 Edition*. Ottawa: Ministry of Supplies and Services.

Corvalan-Vasquez, O. 1988. "Trends in Technical-Vocational and Secondary Education in Latin America." *International Journal of Educational Development* 8.2: 73-98.

Fagerlind, I. and B. Sjosted. 1990. *Review and Prospects of Educational Planning and Management in Europe*. Mexico and Paris: UNESCO/International Congress on Planning and Management of Educational Development.

Farrell, J. P. 1986. *The National Unified School in Allende's Chile: The Role of Education in the Destruction of a Revolution*. Vancouver: University of British Columbia Press.

_____. 1989a. "Doing Horizontal Intellectual Cooperation: Reflections on a Three Year Experience." Paper presented at the annual meeting of the Comparative and International Education Society. Atlanta, GA.

_____. 1989b. "International Lessons for School Effectiveness: The View from the Developing World." *Educational Policy for Effective Schools*. Ed. M. Holmes, et al. New York and Toronto: Teachers College Press and OISE Press.

_____. 1990. "The Political Meaning of Educational Change in Allende's Chile." *Curriculum Inquiry* 20.3: 95-112.

_____. (in press). "Planning Education: An Overview." *International Encyclopedia of Education*. Ed. N. Postlethwaite and T. Husen. 2nd ed. Oxford: Pergamon.

Farrell, J. P., and S. Heyneman, eds. 1989. *Textbooks in Developing Countries: Economic and Educational Choices*. Washington, DC: The World Bank. EDI Seminar Series.

Farrell, J. P., and J. Oliveira, eds. 1993. *Teachers in Developing Countries: Improving Effectiveness and Managing Costs*. Washington, DC: The World Bank. EDI Seminar Series.

Farrell, J. P., and E. Schiefelbein. 1985. "Education and Status Attainment in Chile: A Comparative Challenge to the Wisconsin Model of Occupational Status Attainment." *Comparative Education Review* 29.4: 490-506.

Fullan, M. 1982. *The Meaning of Educational Change*. Toronto: OISE Press.

Fuller, B. 1986. *Raising School Quality in Developing Countries: What Investments Boost Learning?* Washington, DC: The World Bank.

_____. 1991. *Growing Up Modern: The Western State Builds Third World Schools*. New York: Routledge and Kegan Paul.

Ginsburg, M., ed. 1991. *Understanding Educational Reform in Global Context*. New York: Garland Publishing.

Grindle, M. 1989. "The New Political Economy: Positive Economics and Negative Politics." Development Discussion Paper No. 311. Cambridge, MA: Harvard Institute for International Development.

Hall, E. T. 1985. "Unstated Features of the Cultural Context of Learning." *Learning and Development in a Global Perspective*. Ed. A. Thomas and E. T. Ploman. Toronto: OISE Press. 157-176.

Heyneman, S., J. P. Farrell, and M. Sepulveda. 1978. *Textbooks and Achievement: What We Know*. World Bank Staff Working Paper No. 298. Washington, DC: The World Bank.

Kidd, R. 1973. *How Adults Learn*. 2nd ed. New York: Cambridge.

Klees, S. 1989. "The Economics of Education: A More Than Slightly Jaundiced View of Where We Are Now." *The Prospects for Educational Planning*. Ed. F. Caillods. Paris: UNESCO/International Institute for Educational Planning.

Knowles, M. 1983. *The Adult Learner: A Neglected Species*. 3rd ed. Houston: Gulf Publishing Company.

Lockheed, M., and A. Verspoor. 1990. *Improving Primary Education in Developing Nations: A Review of Policy Options*. Washington, DC: The World Bank.

Machiavelli, N. 1952 [1513]. "The Prince." *Great Books of the Western World. Vol. 23*. Ed. R. M. Hutchins. Chicago: Encyclopedia Britannica Inc.

McGinn, N., E. Schiefelbein, and D. Warwick. 1979. "Educational Planning as Political Process: Two Cases from Latin America." *Comparative Education Review* 23.2: 218-239.

McGinn, N., and S. Street. 1986. "Educational Decentralization: Weak State or Strong State?" *Comparative Education Review* 30.4: 471-490.

Migdal, J. 1987. *Strong Societies and Weak States*. Princeton, NJ: Princeton University Press.

Miles, M. 1987. *Planning and Implementing New Schools: A General Framework*. New York: Center for Policy Research.

Psacharopolous, G., C. Rojas, and E. Velez. 1993. "Achievement Evaluation of Colombia's Escuela Nueva: Is Multigrade the Answer?" *Comparative Education Review* 37.3: 263-276.

Puryear, J. 1993. "Status and Problems of International Education Statistics and Research." Paper presented to the Board on International Comparative Studies in Education. National Academy of Science. Washington, DC.

Reimers, F. 1990. *A New Scenario for Educational Planning and Management in Latin America. The Impact of the External Debt*. Paris: International Institute for Educational Planning.

_____. 1991. "The Impact of Economic Stabilization and Adjustment on Education in Latin America." *Comparative Education Review* 35.2: 319-353.

Rondinelli, D., J. Middleton, and A. Verspoor. 1990. *Planning Educational Reforms in Developing Countries: The Contingency Approach*. Durham, NC: Duke University Press.

Ross, K. N., and L. Mahlick. 1990. *Planning the Quality of Education*. Paris: International Institute for Educational Planning.

Samoff, J. 1993. "The Reconstruction of Schooling in Africa." *Comparative Education Review* 37.2: 181-222.

Schiefelbein, E. 1975. "The Politics of National Planning: The Chilean Case." *Educational Planning* 1.3: 212-230.

_____. 1991. *In Search of the School of the 21st Century: Is Colombia's Escuela Nueva the Right Pathfinder?* Santiago, Chile: UNESCO Regional Office for Education in Latin America and the Caribbean.

Shaeffer, S. 1991. *A Framework for Collaborating for Educational Change*. Paris: International Institute for Educational Planning.

Weiler, H. 1983. "Education, Public Confidence, and the Legitimacy of the Modern State. Is There a 'Crisis' Somewhere?" *Journal of Curriculum Studies* 15.2: 125-142.

Weiler, H. 1988. "The Politics of Reform and Non-reform in French Education." *Comparative Education Review* 35.3: 251-265.

EDUCATION, TECHNOLOGICAL CHANGE AND ECONOMIC GROWTH

Thomas Bailey and Theo Eicher [*]

If you plan for a year, plant a seed,
If for ten years, plant a tree,
If for a hundred years teach the people.
— Kuang Tse 551-479 B.C.

SUMMARY

At one level, the importance of education to economic growth seems obvious. But many questions remain: how much education is needed, who should get it, who should deliver it, how should its delivery be organized, who should pay, who will benefit, and how is education related to other types of economic and social policy? In the past it has been difficult to answer these questions, because, surprisingly, analysts have had trouble explaining why and how education is related to growth and competitiveness. But the last decade has seen new progress in theoretical and empirical work on education and growth. This paper uses current economic thinking about the relationship between education, development, and growth as well as recent developments in educational reform in the U.S. to discuss educational policy in developing

[*] Thomas Bailey is the Director of the Institute on Education and the Economy and an Associate Professor in the Department of Economics, Education, Philosophy and Social Sciences at Teachers College, Columbia University. He holds a Ph.D. in labor economics from MIT. He has served as a consultant to many public agencies and foundations including the U.S. Department of Labor, the U.S. Department of Education, the U.S. Congress Office of Technology Assessment, the Alfred P. Sloan Foundation, the William T. Grant Foundation, and several state and local economic development and educational agencies. He has authored or co-authored books on the employment and training of immigrants and the extent and effects of on-the-job training including his most recent book *The Double Helix of Education and the Economy* which was written with Sue Berryman. Theo Eicher is an Assistant Professor in the Department of Economics at the University of Washington, Seattle. He holds a Ph.D. in Economics from Columbia University. His fields of interest include technology, human capital and trade growth and development.

countries. One of the fundamental conclusions of that research is that the relationship between education and growth cannot be understood in the abstract. Education is not something that can be tacked onto the society and economy regardless of the surrounding conditions. Different conditions require different educational strategies.

Introduction

The importance of education to technological change and productivity is at once obvious and opaque. We would be hard pressed to find someone in the industrialized or developing worlds who would deny the importance of education or human capital accumulation to the economic health of any country. But beneath this apparent unanimity, profound questions and disagreements lurk. How much education is needed, who should get it, who should deliver it, how should its delivery be organized, who should pay, who will benefit, and how is education related to other types of economic and social policy?

In the past it has been difficult to answer these questions because, surprisingly, analysts have had trouble explaining why and how education is related to growth and competitiveness. Does education promote productivity and growth because it prepares a technical and intellectual elite or does it strengthen the economy by reducing fertility and improving health? Some analysts in the U.S. argued that education promoted growth in a capitalist economy by creating a docile and obedient workforce.

But the last decade has seen new progress in theoretical and empirical work on education and growth. One of the fundamental conclusions of that research is that the relationship between education and growth cannot be understood in the abstract. Education is not something that can be tacked onto the society and economy regardless of the surrounding conditions. Different conditions require different educational strategies. This insight, as simple as it may seem, has had profound implications for educational strategies in both industrialized and developing countries. In developing countries, it has exposed the folly of educational systems copied from the U.S. or Europe. In developed countries it has suggested that an education system that was appropriate for the post-World War II economy, may no longer be adequate for current economic, political, and technological conditions. In the U.S., the problem is not that schools have deteriorated, as many politicians have argued, but rather that the economy has changed, leaving the schools behind.

And even more complex, new thinking about education and growth in economics suggests that technological and economic conditions may themselves influence the acquisitions of skills and the accumulation of human capital. (Human capital is endogenous in some of these models.) Thus policy makers cannot simply think of education as a tool which they can use to promote growth. Rather trade and commercial policy can influence human capital accumulation which can in turn influence growth and productivity. This line of thinking suggests that free trade, which most economists in the developed world believe would benefit developing countries, may, in some cases, slow the accumulation of knowledge and human capital.

The purpose of this paper is to use current economic thinking about the relationship between education, development and growth to discuss educational policy in developing countries. We first discuss recent developments in the economic theory that link growth and competitiveness to education. We then present the insights derived from the theory for educational and economic policy in developing countries. The subsequent section of the paper discusses relevant economic and educational changes now taking place in the U.S. We end with a summary and conclusions.

Economic Theory, Growth and Education

The promotion of education and training has been a staple of economic development policy for decades. And the importance of education to growth and education in the developed world has also long been recognized. Historians argue that early public education in the U.S. helped launch an era of U.S. economic hegemony. In 1983, the profoundly influential publication *A Nation at Risk*, (U.S. Commission on Excellence in Education 1983) blamed rising trade deficits and stagnant standards of living on a deteriorating U.S. education system. Seven years later, the Commission on Skills in the American Workforce (1990) argued that the country had a "choice" between two future paths. One involved high levels of education, high skills, and rising standards of living, while the other was based on low wages and low skills, and would lead to increasing inequality and a deterioration of the average standard of living. Business people and educators argued that the German and Japanese success in export markets was due to their apparently superior education systems.

Empirical evidence developed over many years has confirmed the importance of both education and technology to economic growth (see Mowery and Rosenberg 1989; Denison 1985; Benhabib and Spiegel 1992; and Mankiw, Romer and Weil 1992). And hundreds of studies have shown that individual earnings rise with education. On a cross country basis, a one-year increase in schooling augments wages by between 5 to 25 percent, after allowing for other factors (World Bank 1991, table 3.2).

But why and how does education promote growth and development? Most analysts agree increases in health, nutrition and higher labor force participation rates are important reasons why education fosters economic development. In 1890 Alfred Marshall wrote that "health, strength, physical, mental and moral ... are the basis of industrial wealth." But these notions have not been explicitly incorporated into economic theories of growth. For many years, developing countries emphasized the need to train a technological and scientific elite. More recently, many analysts have argued that skill and educational deficiencies among lower level workers directly involved with production and agriculture have been a fundamental block to economic development. Which educational policy is most efficient will clearly depend on the underlying reasons why education promotes growth and on the mechanisms and processes through which education is translated into development and increased productivity.

For most of the period since World War II, economic thinking about growth has been based on what has been referred to as the neoclassical benchmark model, which was developed by Solow (1956, 1957). This model assumed that all capital and labor were homogeneous, thus eliminating any consideration of differences in the quality of labor (and capital) that might arise from education, technology, or other factors. In this model, income *levels* were influenced only by population growth (which was considered exogenous) and the accumulation of physical capital (which resulted from savings). In the absence of constant, exogenous technological change, the model implied that the per capita growth *rate* of national income must approach zero in the long run. The policy implications of this model flowed directly from its basic assumptions—in order to raise per capita income, keep population growth to a minimum and raise the savings rate, which would raise the per capita rate of capital accumulation. Education was nowhere to be seen.

Thus the model was useless for analyzing the effects, to say nothing of the causes, of education. The assumption of homogenous labor excluded any consideration of differential effects of education on labor, and while many analysts believed that education might promote technological innovation, this model assumed that such innovation was exogenous (its causes were not under consideration in the model).

Moreover, the earliest empirical tests of the Solow model, so-called growth accounting exercises (Solow 1957; Abramowitz 1956; Denison 1961), suggested that most of the growth in output could not be explained by population growth and the accumulation of capital.

Abramowitz labeled the unexplained "residual" responsible for most of the growth in output, "The Economists Index of Ignorance" (later it received the more neutral term the "Solow Residual"). Discouraged by the simplistic policy implications and the weak empirical support, analysts turned their attention to exploring the components of the Solow Residual to explain economic growth.[1] Early attempts by Solow (1960), Kaldor and Mirrlees (1962) and many others sought to make the model more sophisticated by dropping the assumption of homogeneous capital. They recognized that at any moment, capital included both new and old vintages of equipment and that newer equipment embodied more advanced technology. These so-called vintage capital models enjoyed a period of popularity but the ultimately more successful theoretical extensions of the Solow model were based on dropping the assumption of homogeneous labor.

These investigations, which examined the determinants and importance of human capital investment, were initiated by Schultz (1960) and led to a rich literature on human capital and on-the-job training (Becker 1964; Mincer 1974; and Schultz 1961). By accounting for differences in human capital, economists were then able to account for a much larger share of economic growth.

But the growth accounting exercises were in effect empirical findings without an underlying theoretical explanation. More education was associated with more growth, but why? And there was no consideration of the causes of human capital accumulation (no model took such accumulation as endogenous). Surprisingly, given the consensus about the importance of education, education and endogenous human capital accumulation were not included into formal models until the 1980s. Findlay and Kierzkowski (1983) presented the first model which specifically included endogenous skill accumulation, and documented the importance of the stock of human capital in determining competitiveness, comparative advantage, and the pattern of trade. Subsequently Romer (1986) developed a growth model that explicitly included human capital although in this case human capital was exogenous.[2] Nonetheless, it remained unclear how, and which kind of human capital contributed to economic growth.

The following years saw mounting empirical and theoretical evidence of the importance of technological change and human capital in competitiveness and growth. By the mid to late 1980s studies showed that the level of education (Mankiw, Romer and Weil 1992), the size of the educated work force (Romer 1986, 1989, 1990), the number of patents issued (Grossman and Helpman 1991; Judd 1985), and the size of privately and publicly funded research expenditures in the private and public sector influence not only a country's growth of income, but also its pattern and volume of trade. The approaches of the theoretical literature to explain exactly how human capital contributes to economic growth may be grouped into three rough categories, which are described below.

I) *Education as a separate factor of production*: One approach, developed by Romer (1986), Lucas (1988) and others, suggested that human capital, just like physical capital, can be viewed as a production input which can be accumulated. No explicit relation between human and physical capital and technological change was specified, however. In fact, in this analysis, human capital represented the effective, or average, technological knowledge of an economy, which could be accumulated in a separate education sector, without implied relation to the current standard of technology. The policy implications were that the competitiveness and growth rate of a country are closely tied to the share of its people receiving education and, most importantly the level of educational attainment.

The primary contribution of this line of research was that for the first time, allusions to the important external effects of private human capital accumulation were included into formal models. Society as a whole benefits more than the individual from that individual's education, thus left to their own choices, individuals would invest in less education than was socially optimal. This created a justification for public policy to "internalize" the externality, by subsidizing human capital accumulation.

Internalizing the externality was really just an elegant statement of the conventional public goods justifications for public funding of education in capitalist economies (Friedman 1962). Moreover, since the human capital in these models was included in a highly aggregated form, they were unable to generate insights concerning relative investments in primary, secondary, or tertiary education; how this education should relate to the rate of technological change; or the appropriate government role in subsidizing on-the-job training.

II) *Learning by doing*: Another avenue explored by the theoretical literature based its analysis of human capital on learning by doing. Once again, labor was assumed to be homogeneous, but serendipitous productivity increases were generated as higher volume of output caused production workers to move down the learning curve. Young (1991, 1993); Lucas (1988); Boldrin and Scheinkman (1988); and Stokey (1988), all showed that learning by doing exhibits crucial scale and spillover effects. The benefits of learning by doing were seen to be twofold. The first benefit was the traditional notion (Arrow 1962) that the more volume of a particular good produced, the further labor moved down the learning curve, and the greater the improvement in efficiency and productivity. Second, the more volume of a particular product produced, the more skill useful for the related technology was obtained, making it easier to learn about new, relatively similar, production processes. Increased output therefore led to lower unit costs (although unit costs fell at a decreasing rate), and to important knowledge spillovers, which facilitated the adoption of new technology. Competitiveness and the pattern of trade are then determined by the size of the market (the volume of output in a specific sector) and by the knowledge content of the sector in which learning occurs, leading to important implications for public and commercial policy which will be discussed later.

While learning by doing emphasizes the educational benefits of particular types of production, research also suggests that prior education also influences the effectiveness of learning by doing. Analyses of the relationship between education, training, and earnings show that schooling and learning on the job are complementary. Thus learning by doing will be more effective if it is built on at least a minimal foundation of schooling.

III) *The mutual interaction of technology, human capital, and economic conditions*: The third class of models, rather than viewing education as a simple input into the production process, or emphasizing serendipitous and costless learning by doing, is based on the idea that the invention and adoption of new technology, the accumulation of human capital, and economic conditions are all interdependent—they are endogenous to the model (Nelson and Phelps 1966; Romer 1990; Grossman and Helpman 1991; Eicher 1993).

One hypothesis explaining the empirically observed interaction between technological change and human capital (see, for example, Bartel and Lichtenberg 1987; Davis and Haltiwanger 1991; Mincer 1991) was first proposed by Nelson and Phelps (1966). Specifically, skilled workers are assumed to possess a "comparative advantage" with respect to inventing and adapting new technologies. Nelson and Phelps (1966) suggested that the introduction of a new technology radically transforms the production environment. Skilled workers differ from unskilled in their ability to function in this new environment, since skills enhance the ability to handle new demands created by the new technologies. Nelson and Phelps proceed to rank jobs according to the degree to which they require adaptation to change from unskilled (highly routinized) to highly skilled (involving the necessity "to learn to follow and to understand new technological developments" p. 69).

One implication of this reasoning is that if the technology in a job changes, the quality of skills required must also change. This implies that the first class of models discussed above, which allows for human capital accumulation independent of technological change, is incomplete.

The interaction between human capital accumulation and technological change also relates to the distinction between the determinants of the *adoption* of existing technologies versus the *creation* of new technologies. Learning-by-doing models focus on the cost of adopting a new technique and production process, while the third group of models recognize explicitly that skilled workers also invent the new technologies, which must subsequently be absorbed into production. This distinction between adoption and innovation turns out to be crucial in the discussion of policy implications of the various models.

The proposition that education promotes both adoption and creation of new technology has strong empirical support. Benhabib and Spiegel (1992) show that human capital explains economic growth better when modeled to facilitate the adoption of new technologies, as opposed to being just another input into the production function. Other empirical work by Bartel and Lichtenberg (1987), Mincer (1989, 1991), Davis and Haltiwanger (1991), Juhn, Murphy and Pierce (1993), Berman, Bound and Griliches (1993), and Bound and Johnson (1992) has shown a large degree of complementarily and reciprocity between technological change and human capital. These studies find that a higher rate of technological innovation and adoption increases the demand of skilled relative to unskilled labor.

The new growth models point out another reason why education should be considered endogenous. Schooling itself is also influenced by the current level of technology and quality of skilled labor in teaching.

These interactions between human capital and technological change can be summarized by the following four critical allocation decisions: 1) what share of the population should obtain which skills and how much existing human capital of what quality should be allocated 2) to education, 3) to the invention of new technologies, and 4) to the absorption of innovations.

Thus we have come a long way from the simple notion that more education is better. This third class of models implies that decisions about how much and what type of human capital to accumulate and what resources should be devoted to invention and to absorption cannot be considered independently.

Policy Implications

We have reviewed three classes of recent models of the relationship between education and growth. The first treats education as a distinct factor of production, the second is based on learning by doing, and the third focuses on the mutual interactions between human capital development, invention and adoption of technological change, and economic conditions. We argue that the second and third groups offer specific and important insights for education in both developing and industrialized countries.

Learning-by-doing models are primarily relevant to the adoption of existing technologies, thus they seem particularly important for developing countries, which in general can make great strides by adopting existing equipment and adjusting it to relevant conditions. But we have also argued that schooling and learning on the job are complementary. While learning by doing seems to be a costless by-product of production, its effectiveness in generating competitiveness is influenced by a base level of schooling. Without that base, learning will probably take place, but at a slower rate.

By providing that base education, a country accelerates the dynamic benefits derived from productivity increases resulting from learning by doing. This factor, combined with the increases in health and labor force participation associated with increases in basic education, suggest that, in countries with high levels of illiteracy, there are potentially high social and economic returns to increased investments in primary education. Empirical evidence supports this conclusion. Indeed, numerous studies have shown that the spread of primary education translates into higher agricultural and family enterprise productivity through better absorption of new information and faster adoption of advanced techniques (Welch 1970; Krueger 1991). In Peru, for example, it has been estimated that the return to an additional year of primary education for self-employed women in the textile sector is 33 percent (World Bank 1990).

Thus, on the most basic level, the empirical evidence suggests that during the early stages of the development process, primary education should receive the most resources to develop a critical level of basic skills. However, a cursory examination of government policies suggests that the empirical evidence concerning returns to primary education are too often neglected. For example, while Brazil spends 69 percent of its public education budget on primary education, only 9 percent is spent on secondary but 23 percent on tertiary education. In addition, only 23 percent of all elementary schools received text books in the first grade in the early 1980s. In Chile, Costa Rica, the Dominican Republic, and Uruguay, the top fifth of the income distribution receives more than 50 percent of the subsidies for tertiary education, the poorest fifth receives only 10 percent (World Bank 1990).

The learning-by-doing model suggests that there are important learning benefits to large volume production in strategic areas. This creates a link between general economic and trade policy and human resource development. By subsidizing output, countries can try to promote larger volume production in order to achieve resulting benefits of learning by doing.

But which sector should be subsidized? Given that technological innovations take place all the time, Young (1991) has shown that subsidizing the sector with high knowledge content to be more effective in creating comparative advantage. Such a policy would move production into more skill intensive goods, and prepare the labor force more effectively for the advent and introduction of a new technology. The country with the largest market and most aggressive policy for moving production into high tech sectors (which tend to offer more opportunities for learning) would thus possess a comparative advantage in high tech goods. Active commercial policy could steer the economy in the same direction, and could either create even larger markets and comparative advantage, or accelerate the speed with which a country catches up to more advanced nations.

One policy implication of this is that trade should be managed so as to increase the market size. Even if an imported good is cheaper today than a domestically produced good, relying on the import will reduce the domestic producers' market share and thwart its ability to benefit from economies of scale. Temporary protection may allow the comparatively disadvantaged industry to exploit economies of scale, lowering its per unit cost to such an extent that it may become an exporter of the good in the future. This argument is especially relevant to developing economies, as free trade in the presence of economies of scale may simply consolidate the position of the technological leader. This is an argument for so-called Strategic Trade Policy, which influences the terms of trade of a targeted industry in the "right" direction in order to establish a comparative advantage.[3] This approach implies "picking winners" in international competition. Only industries with high growth potential and high learning potential ought to be targeted.

Basic education and learning from experience are, by themselves, not adequate to support extensive innovation of technology to achieve technological leadership. Innovation must involve tertiary education, not only because post-secondary institutions supply the technical and scientific personnel who can carry out innovations, but because significant amounts of innovation actually take place in university labs. This was the thinking behind the earlier popularity of manpower planning in developing countries, which emphasized the development of a cadre of high level technicians, engineers, and scientists.

112

The third category of models discussed above, has clearly pointed out the problems with this policy prescription. The education of a high-level scientist population must be in relation to the capabilities of a country to absorb the technological innovations, on the one hand, and the stock of scientists on the other. "Overinvestment" in tertiary education can be detrimental to a country's economic growth, if it stands in no relation to the country's technological capabilities, and thus leads to underemployment of high-skilled labor. An emphasis on tertiary education without an adequately educated mass population, for example, may lead to a glut of frustrated university students (see, for example, the Philippines).

Indeed, the manpower planning approach to train high-level personnel has not been effective, and most analysts now agree that the returns to expensive (usually publicly funded) tertiary education in developing countries are not large enough to warrant excessive effort (Psacharopoulos and Woodhall 1985). Even if developing countries can innovate technologically, an adequate base of education among the general population is still required to adopt those innovations. Without access to huge markets that would allow long learning curves, an uneducated workforce cannot make effective use of innovations, homegrown or not.

Furthermore, the Japanese experience especially has shown that much innovation takes place gradually as workers try to solve small problems. This process, which might be called "innovating by doing," can effectively use production workers if they have the skills and understanding to make a contribution. This source of innovation is not available with an uneducated workforce.

Any accumulation of cutting edge technological know how must be carried out in relation to the production and technological possibilities of a country (and vice versa). Studies have confirmed that an exceedingly aggressive policy of adopting and advancing technology without the appropriate level of human capital can slow growth (see Young's (1992) comparison of Singapore and Hong Kong). Young's empirical study has shown that an economy's attempts to leapfrog technologies, (i.e., adopt new technologies without having generated the prerequisite human capital) is not a strategy which utilizes resources efficiently.

U.S. Education Reform and Insights for Developing Countries

Recent economic theories that relate education to economic growth therefore have a variety of implications for economic, trade, and educational policy in developing countries. But recent developments in the industrialized world also provide important insights for educational planners.

Ironically, while theory has exposed the learning and educational benefits of large volume production for developing countries, many industrialized countries, especially the U.S., are trying to adjust their production strategies so that they can produce much smaller quantities of particular products efficiently and rapidly. This argument, developed by Piore and Sabel (1984) and many others, contrasts mass production to flexible production.

Mass production depends on large volume production of identical or similar items to recoup the fixed cost of automation and engineering and to maximize the time during which the workforce is operating near the optimal point on the learning curve. Mass production generally involves detailed planning and engineering by a cadre of highly educated technical and professional personnel. But these planners try to simplify or "dumb down" the jobs of production workers. The assembly line with highly fragmented and repetitive jobs is the paradigmatic example of mass production. Mass production does involve sophisticated equipment and production workers do need a minimal level of education, but these skill demands are not high and the large volume allows maximum operation of the learning curve.

Mass production was particularly successful in the U.S. with its gigantic internal market. Moreover, the American education system was well suited for the skill demands of the mass production approach. The U.S. has, by international standards, very high quality university and especially post-graduate education to prepare the scientific, technological, and professional leadership. But the quality of education received by the three quarters of the population that does not graduate from college or university is of much lower quality than the equivalent levels of education in many European and Asian countries, implying that U.S. workers in comparison to these foreign counterparts learned a larger share of the required skills on the job. Thus the logic of learning-by-doing models applied to the educational needs of production workers while the models that emphasized the interdependence of education and technological innovation were most relevant to the training of higher level personnel.

But economic and technological changes have undermined the basis of the mass production system. Much more intensive international competition and faster changes in products and technologies have greatly reduced opportunities for seemingly endless production of standardized goods using unchanging processes. The learning curve has much less time to operate. Certainly the need for high level technical personnel remains. Indeed it has intensified. But the low quality education of production workers has now become a greater liability for the U.S. system. Other industrialized countries that never had the luxury of the U.S. mass market were never as dependent on learning by doing based on high volume production. This may explain why their non-university education systems are stronger than the U.S. system.

Thus in the U.S., there is a growing realization that much of the workforce is not adequately educated. In past years, high school graduates could get reasonably well-paid unionized jobs that could support a moderate middle-class lifestyle. But in the last 15 years, the real earnings of high school graduates have fallen sharply (Levy and Murnane 1992; Katz and Murphy 1992; Bound and Johnson 1992).

One response to the educational crisis for those students who do not go on to four year colleges has been the reform of the content and curriculum of secondary school. This involves a shift from a didactic pedagogy based on the transmission of information from teacher to student, to what is referred to as a student-centered approach which emphasizes inquiry and discovery on the part of the student.[4] Rather than having teachers lecture to students, a student-centered strategy is based on group projects with open-ended or ambiguous outcomes which facilitate the understanding and application of underlying concepts. There is also a strong current in this reform movement that emphasizes the value of guided internships or apprenticeships in which students have an opportunity to apply school-learned concepts in realistic settings.

A fundamental notion that underlies these school reform movements is that the U.S. is moving into a more dynamic and competitive economy in which learning by doing based on primary or low-quality secondary education is no longer adequate. This puts a greater burden on the education system to produce graduates who can operate in more ambiguous, faster-changing, and less structured environments. Thus we are expecting many more workers to be effective in the types of activities previously carried out by college graduates. These added educational objectives can either be accomplished by sending more students to university or by reforming secondary schools (certainly the most effective strategy will involve a combination of these two approaches). The third class of models discussed above previously focused our attention on tertiary education; the current reforms in the U.S. suggest that some of the objectives that we look for in tertiary education may also be achieved in secondary schools.

What does this imply for developing countries? One possibility is that these countries focus their efforts on capturing those markets that allow high volume production. Certainly such markets still exist and possess significant growth potential in developing countries. The high volume production will allow workers to learn, but if countries focus on traditional labor intensive industries such as apparel and shoes, there will be few benefits to knowledge spillovers. Thus developing countries must target high volume industries with good potential for learning. The policy implications of this approach involve a refocus on primary education, avoidance of overinvestment in tertiary education, and appropriate trade and commercial policy to promote large volume production in specific sectors in order to exploit the learning curve.

But secondary school reform may offer a middle path that would allow developing countries to lay the groundwork to compete in more sophisticated markets without necessarily increasing their emphasis on costly tertiary education. This would still require a solid base of primary education, but it would put less reliance for human capital development on the learning curve generated by high volume production.

Summary and Conclusion

The competitiveness of a firm, an industry, and a nation is related to the mix of primary, secondary, and tertiary education and how that interacts with the level of development and the state of technology. The theories that we have reviewed suggest that a government may play a crucial role in enhancing and allocating the stock of human capital in the economy. Primary education enhances nutrition and health, increases the rate of return in the traditional sectors, and facilitates learning. It is also the foundation for moving to a stage of development where, with expanded secondary education, more and more techniques can be adapted from a technological leader. Comparative advantage, technological leadership and economic growth are most aggressively influenced by a nation's or firm's ability to absorb and advance new technologies, which requires the mastery of previous technologies, a highly skilled workforce, and a large enough stock of scientists and engineers. Here traditionally, the interaction between technological change and accumulation of human capital in the tertiary sector are central. We have argued that trends in school reform in the U.S. suggest that secondary schools could also play a large role in this last objective.

Public policy must have a national and an international focus. First, the government must establish reasonable priorities for the distribution of funds based on the rates of return, and stages of development. On the most basic level, it makes little sense to attempt to be a high-tech exporter and to subsidize heavily tertiary education when primary education is still insufficient. The empirical and theoretical literature suggests that the correct mix of educational and industrial subsidies, at each state of development, is crucial.

The above analysis suggests that strong emphasis ought to be placed on the accumulation of human capital, but not without relation to the existing industrial and technological state of development. Important and cheap advances in human capital can be achieved through learning by doing and targeting both high growth and high-tech industries, if the movement along an industry's learning curve can be accelerated, especially if it occurs in high knowledge content sectors. The theoretical literature suggests that these benefits may be achieved through commercial policy, adjustments in the terms of trade, and subsidies for targeted industries. We have also suggested that appropriate education and job training are needed as a foundation for more effective learning by doing.

As a first step, developing countries should try to capture mass markets in industrialized as well as developed countries. The products that can serve these markets have less demanding skill requirements, they can take advantage of the lower wage levels in developing countries, and the process of production itself generates human capital development through the learning curve. But taking this approach in effect simply follows that path taken by industrialized countries—mastery of standardized products and eventual concentration on more sophisticated and varied goods and services. And the benefits of this approach will be minimal if the products that are produced have little positive spillover effects. Moreover, unlike the industrialized countries, today's developing countries have the experience of those industrialized countries from which they may benefit. While it is unrealistic for developing countries to compete directly in the most advanced markets, improved education does offer an opportunity to build the foundations of economies that are less dependent on basic standardized items. But the key to this is not to try to copy the tertiary systems of the industrialized world, although a solid tertiary system is certainly necessary. Better opportunities lie in a variety of alternative policies including a strong emphasis on primary education, an increase in the quantity and quality of secondary education, and new departures in trade and commercial policies.

NOTES

1. It should be noted that the subsequent developments in trade theory, and the subsequent policy implication, which emphasized the importance of free trade and condemned distortions of prices caused by trade restrictions, were based on the neoclassical benchmark model. With the advent of the new growth theory in the 1980s, which included in the analysis factors such as economics of scale, human capital, learning-by-doing spillovers, and endogenous technological change, economists started to consider the role that strategic trade policy might play in promoting economic development.

2. See Berryman and Bailey (1992) for a full discussion of this approach and the broad policy that is aimed at achieving it.

3. Often this argument is confused with the classic infant industry protection argument, which neither assumes increasing returns to scale, nor knowledge spillovers.

4. See Berryman and Bailey (1992) for a full discussion of this approach and the broad policy that is aimed at achieving.

BIBLIOGRAPHY

Abramowitz, M. 1956. "Resources and Output Trends in the U.S. since 1870." Occasional Paper 52 NBER, New York.

Arrow, Kenneth J. 1962. "The Economic Implications of Learning by Doing." *Review of Economic Studies* 29: 155-173.

Bartel, P. Ann, and Frank R. Lichtenberg. February 1987. "The Comparative Advantage of Educated Workers in Implementing New Technology." *Review of Economics and Statistics* 69: 1-11.

Becker, Gary S. 1964. *Human Capital*. New York: Columbia University Press.

Benhabib, Jess, and Mark Spiegel. October 1992. "The Role of Human Capital in Economic Development." C. V. Starr Center for Applied Economics, New York University, Economic Research Report RR# 92-46.

Berman, Eli, John Bound, and Zvi Griliches. January 1993. "Changes in the Demand for Skilled Labor within U.S. Manufacturing Industries." NBER Working Paper No. 4255.

Berryman, Sue E., and Thomas R. Bailey. 1992. *The Double Helix of Education and the Economy*. New York: Institute on Education and the Economy, Teachers College, Columbia University.

Boldrin, Michele, and Jose A. Scheinkman. 1988. "Learning by Doing, International Trade and Growth: A Note." *The Economy as an Evolving Complex System Reading*. Ed. Philip W. Anderson, Kenneth J. Arrow and David Pines. Reading, MA: Addison Wesley.

Bound, John, and George Johnson. June 1992. "Changes in the Structure of Wages in the 1980s." *American Economic Review* 82: 371393.

Commission on the Skills in the American Workforce. 1990. *America's Choice: High Skills or Low Wages!* Syracuse, NY: National Center on Education and the Economy.

Davis, Steve, and John Haltiwanger. 1991. "Wage Dispersion within U.S. Manufacturing Plants, 1963-86." *Brookings Papers of Economic Activity*, Special Issue: 115-180.

Denison, Edward F. 1961. *Sources of Economic Growth in the U.S.* New York: Committee of Economic Development.

_____. 1974. *Accounting for U.S. Economic Growth: 1929-1969.* Washington, DC: Brookings Institution.

_____. 1985. *Trends in American Economic Growth: 1929-1982.* Washington, DC: Brookings Institution.

Eicher, Theo S. 1993. "Interaction Between Endogenous Technological Change and Endogenous Human Capital." Columbia University, mimeo.

Findlay, Ronald, and Henryk Kierzkowski. December 1983. "International Trade and Human Capital." *Journal of Political Economy* 91: 957-978.

Friedman, M. 1962. *Capitalism and Freedom.* Chicago, Illinois: University of Chicago Press.

Grossman, Gene M., and Elhanan Helpman. 1991. *Innovation and Growth in the Global Economy.* Cambridge, MA: MIT Press.

Judd, Kenneth L. May 1985. "On the Performance of Patents." *Econometrica* 53: 567-585.

Juhn, Chinhui, Kevin M. Murphy, and Brooks Pierce. June 1993. "Wage Inequality and the Rise in Returns to Skill." *Journal of Political Economy* 101: 410-442.

Kaldor, Nicholas, and James A. Mirrlees. 1962. "A New Model of Economic Growth." *American Economic Review*: 117-192.

Katz, Lawrence F., and Kevin M. Murphy. June 1992. "Changes in Relative Wages, 1963-1987: Supply and Demand Factors." *Quarterly Journal of Economics* 107: 35-78.

Krueger, Alan B. August 1991. "How Computers Have Changed the Wage Structure." Princeton University, mimeo.

Levy, Frank, and Robert Murnane. September 1992. "U.S. Earnings Levels and Earning Inequality." *Journal of Economic Literature* 30: 1333-1382.

Lucas, Robert E. February 1988. "On the Mechanics of Economic Development." *Journal of Monetary Economics* 22: 2-42.

Mankiw, N. Gregory, David Romer, and David N. Weil. May 1992. "A Contribution to the Empirics of Economic Growth." *Quarterly Journal of Economics* 107: 407-437.

Marshall, Alfred. 1946. *Principles of Economics.* 8th ed. London: Macmillan.

Mincer, Jacob. 1974. *Schooling Experience and Earnings.* New York: Columbia University Press.

_____. 1989. *Labor Market Effects of Human Capital and of Its Adjustment to Technological Change.* New York: Institute on Education and the Economy, Teachers College, Columbia University.

_____. January 1991. "Human Capital, Technology, and the Wage Structure." NBER Working Paper No. 3581.

119

Mowery, David C., and Nathan Rosenberg. 1989. *Technology and the Pursuit of Economic Growth*. New York: Cambridge University Press.

Nelson, Richard R., and Edmund S. Phelps. May 1966. "Investment in Humans, Technological Diffusion and Economic Growth." *American Economic Review* 56.2: 69-82.

Piore, Michael J., and Charles F. Sabel. 1984. *The Second Industrial Divide: Possibilities for Prosperity*. Basic Books.

Psacharopoulos, George, and Maureen Woodhall. 1985. *Economic Development: An Analysis of Investment Choices*. Washington, DC: World Bank.

Romer, Paul M. October 1986. "Increasing Returns and Long Run Growth." *Journal of Political Economy* 94: 1102-1137.

_____. November 1989. "Human Capital and Growth: Theory and Evidence." NBER Working Paper, No. 3173.

_____. October 1990. "Endogenous Technological Change." *Journal of Political Economy* 98: S71-S102.

Schultz, T. Paul. August 1960. "Capital Formation and Education." *Journal of Political Economy* 68: 571-583.

_____. March 1961. "Investment in Human Capital." *American Economic Review* 51: 1-17.

Solow, Robert M. February 1956. "A Contribution to the Theory of Economic Growth." *Quarterly Journal of Economics* 70.1: 65-94.

_____. August 1957. "Technological Change and the Aggregate Production Function." *Review of Economics and Statistics* 39.3: 312-320.

_____. 1960. "Investment in Technological Progress." *Mathematical Methods in the Social Sciences, 1959*. Ed. K. J. Arrow, S. Karlin and P. Suppes. Stanford: Stanford University Press.

Stokey, Nancy L. 1988. "Learning by Doing and the Introduction of New Goods." *Journal of Political Economy* 96: 701-17.

U.S. Commission on Excellence in Education. 1983. *A Nation at Risk*. Washington, DC: GPO.

Welch, Finis. January 1970. "Education in Production." *Journal of Political Economy* 78: 35-59.

World Bank. 1990. *World Development Report*. New York: Oxford Univ. Press. 79, 81.

_____. 1991. *World Development Report*. New York: Oxford Univ. Press. 57.

Young, Alwyn. June 1991. "Learning by Doing and the Dynamic Effects of International Trade." *Quarterly Journal of Economics* 106: 369-405.

_____. 1992. "A Tale of Two Cities." *NBER Macroeconomic Annual*. Cambridge: MIT Press.

_____. June 1993. "Invention and Bounded Learning by Doing." *Journal of Political Economy* 101: 443-473.

Colección **INTERAMER** / *INTERAMER Collection*

Los estudios y trabajos que integran la colección *INTERAMER* tienen por finalidad poner al alcance del lector temas vinculados con el desarrollo socio-educativo y cultural que se produce en nuestra región. Se dirige tanto a docentes e investigadores como a público en general interesado en la presentación condensada de conocimientos indispensables para la comprensión crítica de problemas de nuestra región. La serie no se limita a una época, a una problemática o a una escuela de pensamiento y presenta obras que forman una biblioteca de consulta y orientación en torno a la educación y la cultura de nuestro tiempo.

The objective of the research and studies that comprise the INTERAMER series is to inform the reader of themes related to socio-educational and cultural developments in the Region. INTERAMER is directed to educators, researchers, and to the general public, all of whom may be interested in a condensed presentation of knowledge that is critical to the understanding of our Region's problems. The series is not limited to an era, a single problem, or to a school of thought, but rather, to a larger extent, presents studies that can be used as consultative material regarding education and culture of our time.

INTERAMER No.

21. *Los sistemas de educación superior en los países del MERCOSUR: Elementos fundamentales y bases para su integración*
Enrique Saravia, ISBN 0-8270-3125-4 $8.00

22. *Un huracán llamado progreso: Utopía y autobiografía en Sarmiento y Alberdi*
Adriana Rodríguez Pérsico, ISBN 0-8270-3158-0 $18.00

23. *Azul... de Rubén Darío: Nuevas perspectivas*
Jorge Eduardo Arellano, ISBN 0-8270-3176-9 $10.00

24. *Indicadores de la comprensión lectora*
Margarita Gómez-Palacio, ISBN 0-8270-3167-X $10.00

25. *¿Pedagogía masculina - educación femenina?*
Winfried Böhm, ISBN 0-8270-3169-6 $12.00

26. *La iconografía musical latinoamericana en el renacimiento y en el barroco: Importancia y pautas para su estudio (Spanish and English)*
Rosario Alvarez, ISBN 0-8270-3177-7 $8.00

27. *Escuela, fracaso y pobreza: Cómo salir del círculo vicioso*
Inés Aguerrondo, ISBN 0-8270-3168-8 $12.00

28. *La educación ambiental se enraiza en el continente*
Marco A. Encalada, ISBN 0-8270-3172-6 $8.00

44. *Etnía y nación, Vol. I*
George de Cerquieria Leite Zarur, comp.,
ISBN 0-2870-3286-6   In Press

45. *Etnía y nación, Vol. II*
George de Cerquieria Leite Zarur, comp.,
ISBN 0-2870-3424-5   In Press

46. *Educación y justicia: Términos de una paradoja*
Pablo Latapí, ISBN 0-8270-3380-X $14.00

47. *Nuevas perspectivas de planificación educativa*
Carlos Múñoz Izquierdo, ISBN 0-8270-3379-6   In Press

48. *Arquitectura vernacular en Panamá*
Julio E. Mora Saucedo, et al., ISBN 0-8270-3278-1 $14.00

49. *Contribución a una pedagogía personalista*
Guiseppe Flores d'Arcais, ISBN 0-8270-3425-3   In Press

50. *El puente de las palabras:*
Homenaje a David Lagmanovich
Ines Azar, ed., ISBN 0-8270-3302-8 $24.00

Para adquirir algunas de estas publicaciones, haga su pedido adjuntando un cheque (personal o bancario) a orden de la OEA a la siguiente dirección:

Departamento de Asuntos Educativos
Centro Editorial
1889 "F" Street, NW
Washington, DC 20006
USA

To order any of these publications, please make your check (personal or bank) payable to the OAS and send to:

Department of Educational Affairs
Editorial Center
1889 "F" Street, NW
Washington, DC 20006
USA

EDUCATION, EQUITY AND ECONOMIC COMPETITIVENESS IN THE AMERICAS:
An Inter-American Dialogue Project

JEFFREY M. PURYEAR
JOSÉ JOAQUÍN BRUNNER
Editors